Taste the Sweetness of Salah

(Unlocking Spiritual Depth Through Prayer)

Aman Maqsood

DEDICATION

This book is dedicated to every soul striving to connect with Allah through the beauty and power of Salah. To those seeking peace in their hearts amidst the turbulence of life, may you find solace and a renewed sense of purpose in your prayer. To the believers who feel distant or disconnected, know that every moment spent in sincere Salah draws you nearer to the endless mercy of Allah.

To my beloved family, whose unwavering love, support, and encouragement have been my strength throughout this journey. Alhamdulillah for every reminder, prayer, and moment of patience you've shown me. Your presence has been a constant source of light and inspiration.

And to the ummah, may this work inspire you to experience the true sweetness of Salah and the deep connection it fosters with our Creator. May Allah guide and protect us all on this path.

CONTENTS

Acknowledgments   i

1   Introduction to Khushu in Salah   1

2   The Importance of Salah in Islam   10

3   Understanding the Concept of Khushu in the Qur'an and Sunnah   20

4   Common Mistakes in Salah   28

5   The Consequences of Heedlessness in Salah   37

6   Practical Steps to Develop Khushu   44

7   Physical Postures and Their Role in Khushu   51

8   The Dangers of Hastiness in Salah   61

9   The Role of Stillness and Calmness in Salah   71

10   The Impact of Salah on Daily Life   81

11   Overcoming Distractions in Salah   91

12   Attaining Consistency in Khushu   102

13   The Prophet's (PBUH) Example in Salah   113

14   The Connection Between Tawheed and Khushu   125

15   Salah and the Afterlife   134

16   Conclusion: Reviving Salah in Our Lives   146

ACKNOWLEDGMENTS

Alhamdulillah, all praise is due to Allah, the Most Gracious, the Most Merciful. Without His guidance, this book would not have been possible. I begin by thanking Allah, who has blessed me with the opportunity to share this work. Every moment of inspiration, every word written, and every understanding comes solely from Him, and every shortcoming is my own.

I would like to express my heartfelt gratitude to my family for their continuous support and patience throughout the development of this book. To my parents, whose prayers have always been my strongest shield, and to my spouse and children, thank you for your understanding and encouragement during the long hours I dedicated to this project. Your love has been my constant source of motivation.

I extend my sincere thanks to the scholars and teachers whose knowledge has guided me on this path. Your dedication to preserving and transmitting the teachings of Islam has been a source of inspiration and direction. May Allah reward you all abundantly for your efforts.

To the readers of my previous works, your feedback, support, and duas have been a driving force behind my continued writing. I pray that this book brings benefit to you and helps deepen your connection with Allah through Salah.

Finally, I would like to thank all those who contributed in any capacity—whether through advice, encouragement, or silent prayers. May Allah reward you all with goodness in this life and the hereafter.

Jazakumullahu khairan to everyone who has been part of this journey. If there is any benefit in this book, it is purely by the mercy of Allah. If there are any mistakes, they are mine alone, and I ask for your forgiveness.

1: INTRODUCTION TO KHUSHU IN SALAH

In the name of Allah, the Most Merciful, the Most Compassionate. All praise belongs to Allah, and we seek His help and forgiveness. We seek refuge with Allah from the evil of our own souls and our bad deeds. Whoever Allah guides, none can misguide, and whoever He misguides, none can guide. I bear witness that there is no deity worthy of worship except Allah alone, without any partners, and I bear witness that Muhammad is His servant and Messenger.

The essence of Islam revolves around the worship of Allah and the submission of one's entire being to Him. Salah, the five daily prayers, is the most significant and regular act of worship, establishing a direct connection between the servant and his Creator. Yet, performing Salah is more than just the physical actions and verbal recitations. The heart, mind, and soul must be aligned with the outward acts, embodying a state of humility and consciousness—what is known as **Khushu.**

Khushu is the very soul of Salah. Without Khushu, Salah may become a mere routine, losing its spiritual essence and transformative power. The Qur'an emphasizes this in Surah Al-Mu'minun, where Allah says: **"Successful indeed are the believers, those who humble themselves in their prayers"** (23:1-2). This verse makes it clear that true success lies in the quality of our prayers, specifically in attaining Khushu.

Khushu is an internal state of the heart that manifests in a deep sense of humility, fear, and love for Allah, allowing the worshiper to focus solely on Him. This presence of heart transforms prayer from an obligation into an intimate conversation with the Creator, fostering spiritual growth and cultivating righteousness. When a person achieves Khushu, Salah becomes a source of strength, guidance, and tranquility.

The absence of Khushu in prayer can have detrimental effects on a

Muslim's spiritual life. The Qur'an warns against heedlessness in prayer in Surah Al-Ma'un: **"So woe to those who pray, but are heedless of their prayer"** (107:4-5). This verse reminds us that simply going through the motions of Salah without engaging the heart leads to a form of worship that is devoid of meaning.

Unfortunately, many of us struggle to maintain focus and concentration during Salah. Our minds drift towards worldly concerns, making it difficult to attain Khushu. Yet, the path to achieving this state is not beyond our reach. It requires conscious effort, discipline, and a sincere desire to connect with Allah.

To develop Khushu, the first step is to recognize its importance and necessity. It is easy to fall into the habit of praying hurriedly, without realizing that we are standing in front of the One who controls our very existence. **"And stand before Allah with humility"** (2:238) — this command from the Qur'an is a reminder of how we should approach every Salah, with a sense of awe and reverence.

Reflecting on the importance of Khushu, we must understand that prayer is not simply a ritual. It is an act of devotion that has the power to transform our hearts and lives. When a person prays with Khushu, they are more likely to leave behind sins, improve their character, and live in a manner that is pleasing to Allah. **"Indeed, Salah prevents immorality and wrongdoing"** (29:45). Salah, when performed with sincerity and focus, serves as a shield against negative behaviors.

The Prophet Muhammad (peace and blessings be upon him) embodied the highest level of Khushu in his prayers. His companions would witness him praying with such deep concentration that they could hear the sound of weeping from his chest, as though he was deeply moved by his connection with Allah. He taught that prayer is not merely a physical act but a profound spiritual experience. His words and actions serve as the perfect example for us to follow in seeking Khushu.

Imam Ibn Qayyim al-Jawziyyah, a renowned scholar, once said, **"The strength of one's prayer is dependent on the strength of one's Khushu. The more a person is in awe of Allah, the more perfect their prayer will be."** This statement highlights that Khushu is not something abstract or unattainable, but rather a state that can be cultivated through sincere effort and mindfulness.

One of the key barriers to achieving Khushu is the lack of understanding of what we recite in prayer. Many Muslims, particularly non-Arabic speakers, perform Salah without comprehending the meaning of the Qur'anic verses or the supplications they recite. This disconnect between the tongue and the heart can prevent us from fully immersing ourselves in prayer. Therefore, it is crucial to learn the meanings of what we are saying in our Salah.

When a worshiper recites Surah Al-Fatihah with understanding, for example, it becomes a heartfelt plea for guidance and mercy. Each verse carries immense significance. **"All praise is for Allah, the Lord of all the worlds"** — this opening verse reminds us that Allah is the Sustainer and Controller of everything. It is a declaration of our dependence on Him and our gratitude for His countless blessings.

Reciting **"You alone we worship, and You alone we ask for help"** (1:5) with understanding brings to the forefront the essence of Tawheed (the oneness of Allah). It is a powerful statement of our submission to Allah's will and our reliance on Him alone. Such awareness during prayer transforms it into a deeply personal and meaningful experience.

Another critical element in developing Khushu is adopting the right mindset before we even begin our Salah. It is important to approach prayer with a sense of preparation and anticipation, rather than rushing into it. The Prophet (peace be upon him) advised his followers to leave behind distractions and approach Salah with a focused mind. Performing Wudu (ablution) properly, wearing clean clothes, and choosing a quiet place for prayer are essential steps in creating the right atmosphere for Khushu.

The Prophet Muhammad (peace be upon him) also emphasized the importance of praying on time. Delaying Salah out of laziness or neglecting its appointed time is a sign of heedlessness. In fact, Allah mentions in the Qur'an: **"So woe to those who pray, but delay their prayers beyond the appointed times"** (107:4-5). A person who values their prayer will make an effort to perform it at its prescribed time, without postponing it until the last possible moment.

By consciously approaching Salah with the intention of connecting with Allah and fulfilling His command, we create an environment where Khushu can flourish. The heart begins to focus solely on Allah, and the distractions of the world fade away. This sense of mindfulness in prayer is what leads to true humility and submission.

Achieving Khushu requires more than just external actions; it requires internal reflection and sincerity. It is important to remind ourselves that when we stand in prayer, we are standing in the presence of Allah, the Almighty. Every time we say "Allahu Akbar," we are acknowledging the greatness of Allah and our smallness in comparison. This realization should fill our hearts with humility and a sense of awe.

The Prophet Muhammad (peace and blessings be upon him) described the prayer as an intimate conversation between the servant and Allah. In a hadith Qudsi, Allah says, **"I have divided the prayer between Myself and My servant into two halves, and My servant shall have what he asks for. When the servant says, 'All praise is due to Allah, the Lord of all the worlds,' Allah says, 'My servant has praised Me.'"** This beautiful interaction highlights the personal nature of Salah and how it is an opportunity to speak directly to Allah.

One of the greatest challenges in attaining Khushu during Salah is the constant bombardment of thoughts and distractions that enter the mind. It is natural for a person's mind to wander, but it is essential to redirect those thoughts and refocus on the prayer. The Prophet Muhammad (peace be upon him) advised his companions to bring their hearts back to their prayer whenever they were distracted. This practice requires patience and perseverance, but over time, it strengthens a person's ability to concentrate during Salah.

A critical technique for maintaining Khushu is understanding that Salah is not just a physical act but an opportunity to seek refuge in Allah from the chaos of life. When standing before Allah, we should remind ourselves that all worldly matters, no matter how important they may seem, are insignificant in comparison to our connection with the Creator. The Qur'an beautifully encapsulates this sentiment in Surah Al-Ankabut, where Allah says, **"Indeed, the life of this world is nothing but play and amusement, but the Hereafter is better for those who are righteous"** (29:64).

When a believer internalizes this reality, the distractions that once seemed overwhelming begin to lose their power. Each moment in Salah becomes a precious opportunity to disconnect from the worldly concerns and reorient the heart towards Allah. The more we remind ourselves of the temporality of this world and the eternal nature of the Hereafter, the easier it becomes to achieve Khushu.

There is a hadith reported by the companion Mujahid, which further emphasizes the dangers of being heedless in prayer. He mentions that the heedless ones, described in the Qur'an as **"those who are neglectful of their prayers"** (107:5), are not simply those who miss their prayers entirely but those who perform it without proper attention or care. This highlights the importance of not only performing the prayer but doing so with the proper mindset, striving to be present with Allah throughout.

Ibn Kathir, a well-known Islamic scholar, explains that the first sign of neglect in prayer is delaying it from its appointed time. He elaborates that those who consistently delay their prayers are among those referred to in this verse. They are heedless not because they do not pray, but because they habitually perform their prayers without prioritizing its importance, often rushing through it at the last moment.

The solution to this neglect lies in discipline. One must make it a priority to perform prayers at their proper times, ensuring that they approach each prayer with the same seriousness and focus they would bring to any other important task in life. When a person prioritizes their Salah, they give it the attention it deserves, fostering an environment where Khushu can take root and grow.

Another essential aspect of developing Khushu is the performance of the physical movements of Salah with calmness and deliberation. The Prophet Muhammad (peace and blessings be upon him) warned against rushing through the actions of Salah. In a famous narration, he saw a man praying quickly, not completing his bowing or prostration properly, and said, **"Go back and pray, for you have not prayed."** This happened three times before the Prophet (peace be upon him) explained to the man that proper prayer requires calmness in each position, ensuring that each action is done with full attention and reverence.

This hadith teaches us that the quality of Salah is more important than its quantity. Rushing through the prayer deprives it of its spiritual benefits and can even invalidate it. Therefore, when performing Ruku (bowing), Sujood (prostration), and Qiyam (standing), each position should be observed fully, giving the heart and mind time to engage with the words being recited.

Properly performing the physical aspects of Salah is not only a sign of reverence but also a means of facilitating Khushu. When each movement is done slowly and thoughtfully, it becomes easier to focus the mind and heart on Allah, allowing for a deeper connection during prayer.

The scholars of Islam, including Ibn al-Qayyim, have also stressed that Khushu is something that can be cultivated with effort and persistence. It is not an automatic state that comes easily but requires a concerted effort on the part of the worshiper. Ibn al-Qayyim explained that the heart, when consistently engaged with Allah, begins to develop a deep sense of awareness and humility. Over time, this leads to a state where Khushu becomes a natural part of Salah.

He further noted that one of the greatest obstacles to Khushu is sin. Engaging in sinful behavior outside of prayer hardens the heart and makes it difficult to focus during worship. Therefore, purifying one's actions and striving to live a righteous life is essential for attaining Khushu. The heart must be clean and free from distractions in order to fully engage with Allah during Salah.

This principle aligns with the hadith of the Prophet (peace and blessings be upon him) in which he said, **"There is a piece of flesh in the body; if it becomes good (reformed), the whole body becomes good. But if it is corrupted, the whole body becomes corrupted. Verily, it is the heart."** (Bukhari and Muslim). This hadith emphasizes the importance of a sound heart in achieving not only a good life but also a meaningful prayer.

As we reflect on the connection between the heart and Salah, it is important to consider the role of sincerity in achieving Khushu. The Arabic term **"Ikhlas"** refers to the purity of intention, performing an act solely for the pleasure of Allah. Without sincerity, no act of worship, including Salah, will be accepted. Allah mentions in the Qur'an: **"And they were not commanded except to worship Allah, being sincere to Him in religion"** (98:5).

Ikhlas and Khushu are interconnected. When a person prays with sincerity, they naturally focus more on Allah, their Creator. Their heart becomes less concerned with the opinions of others and more intent on gaining Allah's pleasure. As a result, Khushu begins to manifest, because the heart is focused on fulfilling the purpose of Salah, which is to seek nearness to Allah.

Therefore, before beginning Salah, it is essential to take a moment to renew one's intention. This simple act of mental and spiritual preparation can have a profound impact on the quality of prayer. When a person consciously dedicates their prayer to Allah alone, the distractions of the world become less significant, and the heart becomes more engaged in the act of worship.

The process of attaining Khushu is also linked to having a proper understanding of who Allah is. The more a person understands the attributes and greatness of Allah, the more they will be able to humble themselves before Him in prayer. One of the reasons people fail to achieve Khushu is that they have a limited understanding of Allah's majesty and mercy.

Reflecting on the names and attributes of Allah is a powerful way to increase humility and focus in Salah. For example, understanding Allah as **Al-Rahman** (The Most Merciful) and **Al-Ghaffar** (The Forgiving) reminds the worshiper that they are standing before a Lord who is full of mercy and forgiveness. This realization brings about a sense of gratitude, awe, and reverence, which enhances the quality of the prayer.

Additionally, remembering Allah's power and control over all things helps the worshiper recognize their own dependence on Him. Knowing that Allah is **Al-Malik** (The King) and **Al-Qadir** (The All-Powerful) instills a sense of humility and submission. As a result, the heart becomes more inclined towards Khushu, and the prayer transforms into a moment of sincere devotion.

Another critical element in achieving Khushu during Salah is recognizing the profound opportunity it offers: direct communication with Allah. Many scholars have emphasized that during Salah, a person is in a private audience with their Creator. The Qur'an refers to this closeness, stating, **"And when My servants ask you about Me, indeed I am near. I respond to the supplicant when he calls upon Me"** (2:186). This verse serves as a reminder that Allah is always near, especially during Salah, and that He listens to and responds to the worshiper's pleas.

This intimate connection should instill a sense of reverence and humility in the worshiper. When a person stands in Salah, they are not merely performing a ritual—they are engaging in a direct conversation with Allah. Recognizing this transforms the entire experience, encouraging the worshiper to focus deeply on their words and actions, knowing that Allah is aware of every movement, thought, and intention.

Furthermore, reflecting on the fact that Allah Himself has prescribed this act of worship for the benefit of His servants helps to cultivate gratitude. The act of Salah is a divine gift, a means of purification, and an opportunity for the believer to draw closer to Allah. With this understanding, each bow and prostration takes on new meaning, and the worshiper is more likely to experience Khushu.

One of the great benefits of Khushu is the impact it has on a person's overall spiritual life. Salah, when performed with true humility and concentration, becomes a means of spiritual elevation. It is through Khushu that a person experiences a deeper connection with Allah, which in turn strengthens their faith and reliance upon Him in all aspects of life.

This spiritual benefit is not limited to the moments of Salah itself but extends far beyond. When a person achieves Khushu in their prayer, they begin to carry that sense of mindfulness and humility into their daily life. The effects of a meaningful Salah are evident in the way a person interacts with others, approaches challenges, and maintains patience in times of difficulty.

The Prophet Muhammad (peace be upon him) emphasized the transformative power of Salah when he said, **"The first thing a person will be called to account for on the Day of Judgment is their Salah. If it is found to be sound, the rest of their deeds will be sound"** (Tirmidhi). This hadith highlights the central role that Salah, and by extension Khushu, plays in shaping a person's character and their ultimate success in the Hereafter.

Developing Khushu requires more than just focus during the moments of prayer—it is a lifelong effort to maintain mindfulness of Allah in all aspects of life. The concept of Khushu is not limited to Salah but extends to a state of awareness that permeates a person's entire existence. A person who is constantly aware of Allah's presence is more likely to develop Khushu in their prayers.

One of the ways to foster this awareness is by engaging in regular remembrance of Allah (dhikr) outside of Salah. The Qur'an encourages believers to remember Allah frequently, saying, **"O you who have believed, remember Allah with much remembrance"** (33:41). This act of constant remembrance helps to soften the heart, making it more receptive to the presence of Allah during Salah.

Moreover, engaging in dhikr throughout the day serves as a reminder of Allah's majesty and mercy, reinforcing the connection that a person builds in Salah. As a result, when the time for prayer arrives, the heart is already inclined towards mindfulness, and it becomes easier to focus and achieve Khushu.

One of the greatest obstacles to achieving Khushu in Salah is the influence of the Shaytan. The Prophet Muhammad (peace be upon him) warned of the devil's attempts to distract worshipers, stating that Shaytan whispers to them during their prayer, attempting to divert their attention away from Allah. This spiritual struggle is something every believer must face, and it requires a conscious effort to overcome.

To protect oneself from these distractions, the Prophet (peace be upon him) recommended seeking refuge in Allah from Shaytan before beginning Salah. This is done by saying, **"A'udhu billahi min ash-shaytan ir-rajim"** (I seek refuge with Allah from the accursed devil) at the beginning of each prayer. By doing so, the worshiper asks Allah to shield them from the influence of Shaytan, allowing them to focus on their prayer.

In addition to seeking refuge in Allah, it is also helpful to understand the tactics Shaytan uses to distract a person during Salah. He often plants thoughts of worldly concerns—work, family, or future plans—in the mind of the worshiper. Recognizing these thoughts for what they are can help a person refocus their attention and return to the prayer with renewed concentration.

A practical way to increase Khushu during Salah is by varying the surahs and supplications recited. The Prophet Muhammad (peace be upon him) often recommended reciting different verses of the Qur'an in each prayer, rather than repeating the same ones. This keeps the mind engaged and prevents the worshiper from falling into a routine that might become monotonous.

Additionally, reflecting on the meaning of the verses being recited can significantly enhance Khushu. For example, when reciting Surah Al-Fatihah, one should ponder the praise of Allah, His mercy, and the supplication for guidance. Similarly, the verses recited in Ruku and Sujood should be understood and reflected upon. This engagement with the Qur'an transforms the recitation from mere words into a deep, meaningful dialogue with Allah.

The Prophet Muhammad (peace and blessings be upon him) also encouraged worshipers to prolong their Ruku and Sujood. In these moments, the heart is closest to Allah, and it is an ideal time to engage in personal supplication, asking Allah for guidance, forgiveness, and mercy. By extending these moments and sincerely communicating with Allah, the worshiper can cultivate a deeper connection with their Creator, further enhancing Khushu.

The importance of Khushu cannot be overstated, as it is one of the defining characteristics of the believers mentioned in the Qur'an. Allah says, **"Successful indeed are the believers. Those who offer their prayers with humility and submissiveness (Khushu)"** (23:1-2). This verse highlights the fact that success, both in this life and the Hereafter, is linked to the quality of a person's Salah and the level of Khushu they are able to achieve.

This success is not only spiritual but also practical. A person who performs their Salah with Khushu is more likely to lead a life of discipline, patience, and mindfulness. They are more conscious of their actions and more aware of the impact their deeds have on their relationship with Allah and with others. As a result, they are more likely to avoid sinful behavior and to strive for excellence in all aspects of their lives.

The attainment of Khushu is, therefore, a goal that every believer should strive for, as it not only enhances their prayer but also transforms their character and their approach to life. The benefits of Khushu are far-reaching, impacting every area of a person's life and bringing them closer to Allah.

The Prophet Muhammad (peace be upon him) also emphasized the significance of performing Salah at its appointed times as a means of achieving Khushu. The Qur'an commands, **"Indeed, prayer has been decreed upon the believers a decree of specified times"** (4:103). Praying on time reflects a sense of discipline and dedication, demonstrating that a person's priority is to obey Allah's commands above all else.

When Salah is delayed or rushed, it often reflects a lack of seriousness about the act of worship. To achieve Khushu, a person should approach Salah with the same seriousness and preparation they would bring to any important task. This means setting aside time, removing distractions, and mentally preparing oneself to stand before Allah.

Praying at the earliest possible time allows the worshiper to give their full attention to the prayer, without the pressure of other obligations. It creates a sense of calm and tranquility, which is essential for achieving Khushu. When a person rushes through their prayer, they often miss out on the spiritual benefits and the opportunity to truly connect with Allah.

Finally, one of the most effective ways to develop Khushu is by consistently making du'a (supplication) to Allah, asking Him to grant focus and humility in prayer. The Prophet Muhammad (peace be upon him) would often make supplications asking for sincerity, focus, and dedication in worship. One such du'a is, **"O Allah, help me to remember You, to give thanks to You, and to worship You in the best manner"** (Tirmidhi).

This du'a is a reminder that achieving Khushu is ultimately a gift from Allah. While a person can take steps to increase their focus and concentration, it is Allah who grants success in worship. Therefore, it is essential to regularly seek His help, asking Him to purify the heart and make it inclined towards His remembrance.

By making du'a consistently, a person reinforces their intention to achieve Khushu and acknowledges their dependence on Allah's guidance and mercy. With sincerity, effort, and reliance on Allah, every believer can take steps towards attaining Khushu and experiencing the profound benefits that come with a meaningful and heartfelt Salah.

2: **THE IMPORTANCE OF SALAH IN ISLAM**

Salah holds a central position in Islam, serving as the cornerstone of a believer's faith. It is the most emphasized act of worship in the Qur'an, and its importance cannot be overstated. Salah is one of the five pillars of Islam, and it is the first act of worship that a person will be asked about on the Day of Judgment. The Prophet Muhammad (peace be upon him) said, "The first thing a person will be asked about on the Day of Judgment is their Salah. If it is sound, the rest of their deeds will be sound. If it is corrupt, the rest of their deeds will be corrupt."

This hadith highlights the immense importance of Salah in shaping the believer's spiritual state. Salah is not merely a physical act, but it represents the submission of the heart and soul to Allah. A person's commitment to prayer reflects their commitment to Allah. This daily act of worship becomes a means of purifying the soul, strengthening faith, and drawing nearer to Allah.

The significance of Salah is reinforced by its mandatory nature. Allah, in His infinite wisdom, prescribed Salah five times a day. These five prayers serve as intervals of spiritual renewal throughout the day. They are moments in which the believer detaches from worldly affairs and turns their attention entirely to their Creator. Each prayer serves as a reminder of the believer's ultimate purpose in life: to worship Allah and seek His pleasure.

The importance of Salah is further illustrated by its direct connection to success. Allah, in Surah Al-Mu'minun, says, **"Successful indeed are the believers, those who humble themselves in their prayers."** (23:1-2). Here, Allah links success with humility in Salah. This success is not confined to this world, but extends to the Hereafter. Through Salah, a believer attains spiritual success, which transcends material wealth or worldly accomplishments. The true measure of success in Islam is found in a person's relationship with Allah, and Salah is the means by which that relationship is nurtured and strengthened.

Moreover, Salah is a reminder of the temporary nature of this world and the eternal nature of the Hereafter. Each prayer serves as a moment to realign one's priorities and focus on what truly matters. The Qur'an reminds us, **"And seek help through patience and prayer, and indeed, it is difficult except for the humbly submissive [to Allah]."** (2:45). This verse emphasizes that Salah is not just an act of worship but also a source of strength for the believer. It is through Salah that a person finds solace in times of difficulty and patience in the face of challenges.

Salah also plays a transformative role in a believer's character. When a person performs their Salah with sincerity, it instills in them a sense of discipline, humility, and awareness of Allah's presence. This awareness spills over into all aspects of life, affecting the way a person interacts with others and the choices they make. Salah helps to purify the heart and mind, guiding the believer towards righteousness.

A key aspect of Salah is its ability to prevent a person from engaging in sinful behavior. Allah says in the Qur'an, **"Indeed, Salah prevents immorality and wrongdoing"** (29:45). This verse underscores the protective power of Salah. When performed correctly and with sincerity, Salah serves as a shield against evil inclinations. The constant remembrance of Allah through prayer makes a person more conscious of their actions and less likely to fall into sin.

This spiritual transformation is a gradual process, but its effects are profound. Over time, Salah helps to refine a person's character, making them more compassionate, patient, and just. It is through this daily connection with Allah that a person's heart is purified and their conduct is improved.

One of the unique aspects of Salah is that it is a direct command from Allah, given to the Prophet Muhammad (peace be upon him) during the miraculous journey of Al-Isra' wal-Mi'raj. During this journey, the Prophet was taken to the heavens, where he received the command for Salah directly from Allah. Initially, fifty prayers were prescribed, but after multiple requests from the Prophet, Allah reduced it to five, while still granting the reward of fifty prayers.

This incident illustrates the significance of Salah in the eyes of Allah. It is the only act of worship that was commanded directly in the heavens, which signifies its elevated status in Islam. Salah is not just another form of worship—it is the very foundation of a Muslim's relationship with Allah. It is a direct line of communication between the servant and the Creator, and it must be treated with the utmost reverence.

The fact that Allah reduced the prayers from fifty to five, while still granting the reward of fifty, is a mercy and a blessing for the Ummah. It reflects Allah's desire for ease and His immense generosity towards His creation. Salah, therefore, is not a burden but a divine gift, through which the believer can attain closeness to Allah and earn immense rewards.

Salah is not only a personal obligation but also a communal one. The Prophet Muhammad (peace be upon him) emphasized the importance of praying in congregation. He said, "Prayer in congregation is twenty-seven times more rewarding than praying alone" (Bukhari). This hadith underscores the value of communal worship and the spirit of unity that Salah fosters within the Muslim community.

Praying in congregation strengthens the bonds between believers and promotes a sense of brotherhood. It reminds the individual that they are part of a larger Ummah, all of whom are striving towards the same goal: the pleasure of Allah. Congregational prayer also teaches humility, as the worshiper stands shoulder to shoulder with others, regardless of their social status, wealth, or background. In the masjid, everyone is equal in the sight of Allah.

The communal aspect of Salah is particularly evident during Jumu'ah (Friday) prayers, which hold a special significance in Islam. The Prophet (peace be upon him) said, "The best day the sun rises over is Friday" (Muslim). Attending Jumu'ah prayers is obligatory for men, and it serves as a weekly gathering where Muslims come together to worship, seek knowledge, and strengthen their faith. The importance of Jumu'ah highlights the role of Salah not only in individual worship but also in building a cohesive and supportive Muslim community.

The five daily prayers are a constant reminder of the believer's purpose in life. Allah says in the Qur'an, **"I did not create jinn and mankind except to worship Me"** (51:56). Salah is the most prominent form of this worship, and it serves as a daily affirmation of the believer's submission to Allah. Each prayer is an opportunity to renew one's intention and reaffirm their commitment to living a life that is pleasing to Allah.

Moreover, Salah provides structure and discipline to a Muslim's life. The five daily prayers are spread throughout the day, ensuring that a believer remains connected to Allah regardless of their worldly activities. This regularity instills a sense of responsibility and time management, as the believer is required to organize their day around their prayers. This discipline is a reflection of the broader Islamic ethos, which encourages balance between worship, work, and other aspects of life.

The timings of the prayers are also significant. They are strategically placed at different intervals of the day, allowing the believer to take breaks from their worldly concerns and refocus on their relationship with Allah. Each prayer serves as a moment of spiritual recharge, enabling the believer to continue their day with renewed energy and a clear sense of purpose.

In addition to its spiritual and communal benefits, Salah also has profound psychological and emotional benefits. It provides a sense of inner peace and tranquility that is unmatched by any other activity. The act of turning to Allah, bowing in submission, and placing one's forehead on the ground in Sujood (prostration) is an expression of complete humility and surrender. This act alone can bring immense comfort to the heart and mind.

Allah describes this state of peace in the Qur'an, saying, **"Verily, in the remembrance of Allah do hearts find rest"** (13:28). Salah is the most direct and powerful form of remembrance (dhikr), and it has the ability to soothe the soul and alleviate stress. In a world filled with distractions, anxieties, and challenges, Salah serves as a sanctuary where the believer can find solace in the presence of Allah.

The act of Salah also encourages mindfulness, as it requires the worshiper to be fully present in the moment. When performed with focus and Khushu, Salah helps to clear the mind of distractions and worries. This mindfulness extends beyond the prayer itself and can have a lasting impact on a person's overall mental well-being.

Salah is also a powerful tool for self-discipline. The regularity of the five daily prayers requires a level of commitment and consistency that strengthens a person's ability to control their desires and urges. By pausing throughout the day to perform Salah, the believer practices self-restraint, delaying their immediate desires in order to prioritize their worship of Allah. This habit of discipline that is cultivated through Salah extends into other areas of life as well, making the individual more resilient against distractions and temptations.

Additionally, Salah teaches a person to be punctual. The Prophet Muhammad (peace be upon him) was known for performing his prayers at their earliest prescribed times, and he encouraged others to do the same. Praying on time is not just about fulfilling a religious obligation—it's a reflection of one's commitment to Allah. It instills a sense of urgency and respect for time, which ultimately helps a person become more organized and efficient in managing their daily responsibilities.

Beyond its immediate benefits, Salah also provides long-term spiritual nourishment. Each prayer is an opportunity for the believer to increase their taqwa (God-consciousness) and enhance their relationship with Allah. The Qur'an repeatedly emphasizes the importance of taqwa in leading a successful and righteous life. Salah serves as a constant reminder of Allah's presence, encouraging the believer to live with integrity, honesty, and kindness in all of their interactions.

One of the most profound aspects of Salah is its ability to foster gratitude within the believer. In each prayer, the worshiper recites Surah Al-Fatiha, which begins with the words, **"Alhamdulillahi Rabbil 'Alamin"** (Praise be to Allah, the Lord of all the worlds). This declaration of praise and gratitude is the foundation upon which the entire prayer is built. By starting the prayer with this acknowledgment of Allah's countless blessings, the believer is reminded to be grateful for all that they have been given.

Gratitude is a key characteristic of a true believer, and Salah provides a daily opportunity to express this gratitude to Allah. The act of bowing in Ruku and prostrating in Sujood are physical manifestations of the believer's humility and thankfulness to their Creator. Through these actions, the worshiper acknowledges their dependence on Allah and their recognition of His mercy and grace.

In addition to fostering gratitude, Salah also cultivates patience. Life is filled with tests and trials, and it is through Salah that a believer learns to face these challenges with patience and perseverance. The act of praying itself requires patience, as it involves a commitment to consistency and focus. Moreover, the supplications made during Salah often revolve around seeking guidance, forgiveness, and strength from Allah, reinforcing the idea that true patience comes from reliance on Him.

Salah is not just a ritual—it is a profound form of communication between the worshiper and Allah. The Prophet Muhammad (peace be upon him) described Salah as **"the coolness of my eyes"** (Nasai), highlighting the comfort and serenity he found in prayer. For the believer, Salah offers a similar experience of closeness to Allah. During each prayer, the worshiper engages in a direct conversation with their Creator, presenting their needs, hopes, and fears.

This connection with Allah is not limited to the words of the prayer itself. The act of Sujood, in particular, is one of the most intimate moments between a servant and their Lord. The Prophet Muhammad (peace be upon him) said, **"The closest a servant comes to his Lord is when he is prostrating"** (Muslim). In Sujood, the believer places their forehead on the ground, symbolizing total submission and humility. This act serves as a reminder that no matter how great or powerful a person may be, they are ultimately dependent on Allah for everything.

Salah also provides the believer with a sense of purpose. Each prayer is an opportunity to refocus on their ultimate goal in life: to worship Allah and attain His pleasure. The repetition of this act throughout the day helps to reinforce this sense of purpose, ensuring that the believer remains on the straight path and does not become distracted by worldly concerns.

An essential part of Salah is Khushu, which refers to the state of humility, concentration, and submission that a person should maintain during prayer. Khushu is the heart of Salah, and without it, the physical actions of prayer become hollow. Allah describes the successful believers as those who are humble in their prayers, saying in the Qur'an, **"Certainly will the believers have succeeded: they who are during their prayer humbly submissive"**

(23:1-2).

Khushu is achieved by focusing the mind and heart on Allah and the meaning of the words being recited in the prayer. It involves shutting out distractions and being fully present in the moment. This level of concentration is not always easy to attain, especially in a world filled with constant noise and interruptions. However, the more a person strives for Khushu, the more they will experience the spiritual depth and transformative power of Salah.

The rewards for achieving Khushu in Salah are immense. The Prophet Muhammad (peace be upon him) said, **"Whenever a Muslim offers a prayer, if he perfects its ablution, humility, and bowing, it will be an expiation for his past sins, as long as they are not major sins"** (Muslim). This hadith highlights the importance of striving for excellence in Salah, not only in its physical aspects but also in the inner state of the worshiper.

While achieving Khushu in every prayer may seem challenging, there are several steps a believer can take to improve their focus and humility during Salah. One of the most effective ways is to understand the meaning of the words being recited. When a person knows the translation and significance of Surah Al-Fatiha, the various tasbeeh (glorifications), and the supplications made during the prayer, they are more likely to engage with the prayer on a deeper level.

Another way to enhance Khushu is to perform each movement of the prayer slowly and deliberately. Rushing through Salah diminishes its impact and makes it difficult to focus. Instead, the believer should take their time, ensuring that each action—whether it is bowing in Ruku or prostrating in Sujood—is done with intention and mindfulness.

In addition to understanding the words and slowing down the movements, a believer can also improve their Khushu by reflecting on the greatness of Allah. Before starting the prayer, they can take a few moments to remind themselves of Allah's infinite power, mercy, and wisdom. This reflection helps to create a sense of awe and humility, making it easier to focus during the prayer.

It is important to remember that Khushu is not just about the external actions of the prayer—it also involves the state of the heart. A person may perform the physical movements of Salah perfectly, but if their heart is distracted or insincere, they will not attain the full benefits of the prayer. Therefore, the believer should constantly strive to purify their heart and intentions, seeking to draw closer to Allah through each prayer.

One of the most common distractions during Salah is the mind wandering to worldly concerns. The Prophet Muhammad (peace be upon him) advised against this, saying, **"A person finishes his prayer and only half, a third, a quarter, or a tenth of it may be recorded for him according to the degree of his Khushu"** (Abu Dawood). This hadith highlights the importance of focus and concentration during prayer. If a person allows their mind to wander, they risk losing out on the full rewards of the Salah.

To combat distractions, the believer should try to prepare mentally and spiritually before starting the prayer. This can be done by performing a proper Wudu (ablution), finding a quiet place to pray, and removing any external distractions. By setting the right environment and mindset, the believer increases their chances of achieving Khushu and experiencing the full spiritual benefits of Salah.

Salah is not only a means of connecting with Allah, but it is also a tool for self-improvement. Each prayer is an opportunity for the believer to reflect on their actions, seek forgiveness for their shortcomings, and make a renewed commitment to living a righteous life. The Qur'an says, **"And establish prayer for My remembrance"** (20:14). This verse reminds us that the primary purpose of Salah is to remember Allah and to keep Him at the forefront of our minds and hearts.

In this sense, Salah serves as a form of spiritual accountability. By regularly standing before Allah in prayer, the believer is reminded of their duties and responsibilities. It is a chance to realign oneself with the teachings of Islam and to seek guidance on how to live a life that is pleasing to Allah. The act of seeking forgiveness during the prayer is particularly significant, as it reflects the believer's awareness of their own shortcomings and their desire to improve.

The Prophet Muhammad (peace be upon him) described Salah as a form of purification, saying, **"If there was a river at the door of one of you, and he bathed in it five times a day, would you notice any dirt on him?" They said, 'Not a trace of dirt would be left.' The Prophet said, 'That is the likeness of the five daily prayers; Allah wipes away the sins by them'** (Bukhari, Muslim). This hadith emphasizes the cleansing power of Salah, both physically and spiritually. Each prayer washes away sins and renews the believer's commitment to Allah.

Salah not only serves as a form of purification but also as a reminder of one's purpose in life. Every time the believer stands for Salah, they are reminded of their ultimate goal: to worship Allah and earn His pleasure. This constant reminder helps to keep a person grounded, preventing them from becoming too attached to the temporary pleasures of the dunya (worldly life). Allah says in the Qur'an, **"Indeed, the prayer prohibits immorality and wrongdoing, and the remembrance of Allah is greater"** (29:45). Through Salah, the believer is constantly reminded to stay away from sinful behavior and to adhere to the path of righteousness.

Moreover, Salah provides a structured rhythm to a believer's day. The five daily prayers are spread out at key intervals, starting with Fajr at dawn and ending with Isha at night. This structure helps a person organize their time and ensures that they are never far from their connection with Allah. The Prophet Muhammad (peace be upon him) emphasized the importance of adhering to the prescribed times for prayer, saying, **"The best of deeds is the prayer at its appointed time"** (Bukhari, Muslim). By prioritizing prayer, the believer places Allah at the center of their life, ensuring that everything else revolves around this central act of worship.

Additionally, the daily prayers serve as a form of spiritual nourishment. Just as the body requires food and water to function properly, the soul requires regular acts of worship to stay healthy. Salah is a source of spiritual sustenance that replenishes the soul and strengthens the believer's connection to Allah. The Prophet Muhammad (peace be upon him) said, **"Between a man and shirk and kufr is the abandonment of Salah"** (Muslim), highlighting the essential role that prayer plays in maintaining one's faith.

Another important aspect of Salah is its ability to foster humility. The physical actions of prayer—such as bowing in Ruku and prostrating in Sujood—are powerful reminders of a person's insignificance before Allah. When the believer places their forehead on the ground during Sujood, they are symbolically acknowledging their dependence on Allah and their total submission to His will. This act of humility is not only an expression of worship, but it also serves to humble the believer in their daily life. By regularly reminding themselves of their status as servants of Allah, the believer is less likely to fall into arrogance or pride.

Humility is a key characteristic of a true believer, and it is something that is cultivated through regular acts of worship like Salah. The Prophet Muhammad (peace be upon him) said, **"Whoever humbles himself before Allah, Allah will raise him in status"** (Muslim). This hadith reflects the spiritual benefit of humility—those who lower themselves before Allah are rewarded with honor and dignity in both this life and the next. Salah, with its emphasis on submission and humility, is a means by which the believer can attain this elevated status.

In addition to fostering humility, Salah also encourages a sense of unity among Muslims. When performed in congregation, Salah becomes a communal act of worship that brings believers together. The Prophet Muhammad (peace be upon him) said, **"The prayer in congregation is twenty-seven times superior to the prayer offered by a person alone"** (Bukhari, Muslim). This hadith highlights the immense reward for praying in congregation, as well as the importance of fostering unity within the Muslim community.

Praying in congregation also serves as a reminder of the brotherhood and sisterhood that exists within the Ummah (Muslim community). When standing side by side in Salah, there is no distinction between rich and poor, young and old, or any other social divisions. Everyone is equal before Allah, and this equality is reflected in the rows of prayer. The sense of unity that is fostered through congregational prayer strengthens the bonds between Muslims and reinforces the idea that they are all part of a larger community working together to please Allah.

Furthermore, congregational prayer provides an opportunity for Muslims to support and encourage one another in their worship. When praying together, believers can benefit from the collective strength and focus of the group, which helps to enhance their own concentration and devotion. The Prophet Muhammad (peace be upon him) said, **"The believer to another believer is like a building whose different parts enforce each other"** (Bukhari, Muslim). Salah in congregation is a reflection of this concept, as it allows Muslims to reinforce one another in their worship and strengthen the collective faith of the community.

In addition to its communal benefits, Salah in congregation also serves as a form of accountability. When praying with others, the believer is less likely to rush through the prayer or become distracted. Instead, they are more likely to perform the prayer with care and focus, knowing that they are part of a group that is collectively striving to please Allah. This accountability helps to ensure that the believer maintains a high level of devotion and sincerity in their worship.

While praying in congregation is highly encouraged, it is also important to remember that Salah is ultimately a personal act of worship. Each individual is responsible for their own prayer, and the quality of their Salah is dependent on their own level of Khushu and sincerity. The Prophet Muhammad (peace be upon him) said, **"Indeed, Allah does not look at your appearance or your wealth, but He looks at your heart and your deeds"** (Muslim). This hadith serves as a reminder that the external actions of Salah are not as important as the internal state of the heart. A person may perform the physical movements of Salah perfectly, but if their heart is not sincere, their prayer will not be accepted by Allah.

This emphasis on sincerity is particularly important when it comes to the intention behind the prayer. The Prophet Muhammad (peace be upon him) said, **"Actions are judged by intentions"** (Bukhari, Muslim). Before starting each prayer, the believer should make a sincere intention to perform the prayer solely for the sake of Allah. This intention should be free from any desire for recognition or praise from others. By purifying their intention, the believer ensures that their Salah is a genuine act of worship that is pleasing to Allah.

Moreover, sincerity in Salah is not just about the intention at the beginning of the prayer—it must be maintained throughout the entire act of worship. The believer should strive to remain focused and present in their prayer, avoiding any distractions or thoughts that may take them away from their connection with Allah. The Prophet Muhammad (peace be upon him) warned against praying in a distracted state, saying, **"A person finishes their prayer, and only a fraction of it is recorded for them, as much as they were focused on"** (Abu Dawood). This hadith highlights the importance of maintaining sincerity and focus throughout the entire prayer.

In order to enhance their focus during Salah, the believer can take several practical steps. One of the most effective ways to maintain concentration is to understand the meaning of the words being recited in the prayer. When a person knows the translation and significance of the various supplications and verses, they are more likely to engage with the prayer on a deeper level. For example, when reciting Surah Al-Fatiha, the believer should reflect on the meaning of phrases such as **"Iyyaka na'budu wa iyyaka nasta'een"** (You alone we worship, and You alone we ask for help). By understanding the meaning of these words, the worshiper can connect with them more deeply and experience a greater sense of closeness to Allah.

Another practical way to enhance focus in Salah is to eliminate external distractions. The Prophet Muhammad (peace be upon him) recommended finding a quiet and clean place to pray, free from any noise or interruptions. This allows the believer to fully concentrate on their worship without being distracted by their surroundings. In addition, performing a proper Wudu (ablution) before prayer helps to prepare the mind and body for Salah, creating a sense of physical and spiritual cleanliness that enhances the experience of worship.

Finally, the believer should approach each prayer with a sense of anticipation and excitement. Salah should not be viewed as a burden or a chore, but as an opportunity to connect with Allah and seek His guidance and mercy. By developing a positive attitude towards prayer, the believer is more likely to approach Salah with enthusiasm and sincerity, making the experience more meaningful and impactful.

In conclusion, Salah is one of the most powerful and transformative acts of worship in Islam. It serves as a means of connecting with Allah, purifying the soul, and fostering a sense of humility and gratitude. Through Salah, the believer is reminded of their purpose in life and is given the strength and guidance to navigate the challenges of the dunya. Whether performed in congregation or individually, Salah is a source of spiritual nourishment that helps the believer maintain a strong connection with their Creator.

By striving for Khushu in each prayer, understanding the meaning of the words being recited, and maintaining sincerity in their intention, the believer can maximize the benefits of Salah. The Prophet Muhammad (peace be upon him) said, **"Pray as if you see Allah, and if you cannot see Him, know that He sees you"** (Bukhari, Muslim). This hadith encapsulates the essence of Salah—it is an intimate conversation with Allah, one in which the believer expresses their submission, gratitude, and reliance on their Creator.

Through regular and sincere Salah, the believer can attain closeness to Allah, spiritual growth, and success in both this life and the Hereafter. As the Prophet Muhammad (peace be upon him) said, **"The first thing a person will be called to account for on the Day of Judgment is their prayer. If it is good, their entire record will be good, and if it is bad, their entire record will be bad"** (Tirmidhi). This hadith serves as a reminder of the central role that Salah plays in the life of a Muslim, and the immense rewards that await those who perform it with sincerity and devotion.

3: UNDERSTANDING THE CONCEPT OF KHUSHU IN THE QUR'AN AND SUNNAH

The concept of Khushu in Salah has its roots deeply embedded in the Qur'an and the Sunnah of the Prophet Muhammad ﷺ. Khushu refers to the state of humility, submission, and complete concentration in prayer. It is a profound internal condition that reflects a believer's total surrender to Allah during Salah. The Qur'an repeatedly emphasizes the importance of Khushu as a core attribute of the believers. In Surah Al-Mu'minun, Allah states, *"Certainly will the believers have succeeded: They who are during their prayer humbly submissive."* (Qur'an 23:1-2). This verse highlights that one of the essential qualities for success in this life and the Hereafter is having Khushu in Salah.

Khushu encompasses both the heart and the body. While the heart is engaged in complete devotion and attentiveness, the body reflects this inward state by demonstrating humility through its movements and stillness. The physical postures of Salah are meant to mirror the internal feelings of submission, creating a perfect harmony between the soul and the body.

The significance of Khushu is further elaborated in numerous hadiths. The Prophet Muhammad ﷺ, whose prayers were the epitome of Khushu, provided the best example for the believers. In one hadith narrated by Abu Hurairah, the Prophet ﷺ mentioned: *"The first thing to be lifted from this Ummah will be Khushu, until you will not see anyone who has Khushu."* (Tirmidhi). This hadith points to the gradual decline of sincere, focused prayers, warning us of a time when Khushu will become rare. The Prophet ﷺ constantly encouraged his companions to safeguard their Salah, ensuring that it is performed with the utmost devotion and presence of heart.

In another hadith, the Prophet ﷺ mentioned: *"Pray as if you see Him, and if you do not see Him, then indeed He sees you."* (Bukhari and Muslim). This profound statement underlines the essence of Khushu, reminding the believer that they are constantly in the presence of Allah, whether they can physically see Him or not. This realization transforms Salah into a deeply spiritual experience, where every movement, word, and thought is directed towards Allah.

Khushu is not simply a ritualistic formality but the lifeblood of Salah. The scholars of Islam have dedicated considerable effort to explain the concept of Khushu, warning against its absence in prayer. One of the explanations offered by the scholars is that the believer should not approach Salah as a burdensome obligation. Rather, it should be seen as a privilege and an opportunity to converse with Allah. Imam Ibn Al-Qayyim, in his famous work *Madarij al-Salikeen*, emphasized the importance of Khushu, stating that Khushu is the foundation of all acts of worship. Without it, Salah becomes hollow and devoid of its true purpose.

The absence of Khushu leads to heedlessness in Salah, which the Qur'an strongly condemns. Allah says in Surah Al-Ma'un: *"So woe to those who pray, but are heedless of their prayer."* (Qur'an 107:4-5). This verse is a stern warning for those who mechanically go through the motions of prayer without any presence of mind or heart. Such individuals may fulfill the external requirements of Salah but are deprived of its spiritual benefits.

When the Qur'an speaks of those who are heedless in their prayers, it refers to those who allow their minds to wander during Salah, focusing on worldly concerns rather than their connection with Allah. The scholars have noted that heedlessness during prayer can take many forms. It can manifest as distractions caused by external factors, such as thinking about daily tasks, or internal distractions, such as self-centered thoughts that detract from one's focus on Allah. This heedlessness is a direct consequence of a lack of Khushu.

The Qur'an repeatedly stresses the importance of safeguarding one's prayer and performing it with sincerity. In Surah Al-Baqarah, Allah reminds the believers: *"And seek help through patience and prayer, and indeed, it is difficult except for the humbly submissive [to Allah]."* (Qur'an 2:45). This verse reflects that maintaining Khushu requires effort and patience. For those who are truly devoted to Allah, however, Salah becomes a source of comfort and ease, rather than a burdensome task.

A striking example of Khushu is found in the life of the Prophet Muhammad ﷺ. His entire approach to Salah was one of utmost reverence and humility. Aisha, the wife of the Prophet ﷺ, reported that when the time for prayer came, he would say, *"O Bilal, give us comfort by calling for prayer."* (Abu Dawood). This statement reflects how Salah was a refuge for the Prophet ﷺ, a time when he could disconnect from the worldly affairs and focus solely on his Lord. Salah was not a mere obligation for him but a source of peace and contentment.

The Prophet's Khushu was not limited to his own prayers but extended to the way he guided others. He frequently corrected the companions who rushed through their prayers or were careless in their movements. For example, a man once came to the Prophet ﷺ and prayed in front of him. After finishing, the Prophet ﷺ said to him, *"Go back and pray, for you have not prayed."* This happened three times, after which the man asked the Prophet to teach him how to pray properly. The Prophet ﷺ then explained the importance of performing each movement with deliberation and tranquility, demonstrating the essence of Khushu.

The legacy of Khushu from the Qur'an and Sunnah is clear: it is a defining characteristic of a true believer and a fundamental element of Salah. The companions of the Prophet ﷺ embodied this principle in their own prayers. Umar ibn Al-Khattab, the second caliph of Islam, was known for his profound Khushu. It was narrated that during his prayers, he would weep so intensely that those standing behind him could hear his sobs. Umar's connection to Allah was so deep that the words of the Qur'an would move him to tears, reminding him of the reality of the Hereafter and the overwhelming mercy of Allah.

This deep sense of Khushu is what distinguished the companions and early Muslims. Their prayers were not confined to ritualistic actions but were filled with meaning, emotion, and devotion. They saw Salah as an opportunity to renew their relationship with Allah, seeking His guidance and forgiveness. This approach to Salah transformed not only their spiritual lives but also their behavior and interactions with others.

Khushu, as illustrated by the lives of the Prophet ﷺ and his companions, is a means of attaining nearness to Allah. The scholars have often remarked that the more a person develops Khushu, the more they will find peace and contentment in their prayers. The physical postures, the recitation of the Qur'an, and the supplications during Salah are all designed to instill a sense of humility and submission. These elements of prayer create a direct connection between the servant and the Creator, allowing the believer to experience the sweetness of faith.

In addition to focusing on the internal aspects of Khushu, the outward elements of Salah are equally important. The Prophet ﷺ emphasized the importance of performing each movement with calmness and precision. Rushing through Salah or performing it hastily without giving due attention to each posture is contrary to the teachings of the Prophet ﷺ. The body's stillness in Salah reflects the heart's tranquility, and both are essential for attaining Khushu.

Attaining Khushu in Salah is not a passive experience but requires a conscious effort on the part of the believer. The scholars of Islam have discussed various methods to enhance Khushu, all centered around creating an environment of concentration and reverence during Salah. One of the most effective ways to develop Khushu is to remember that one is standing before Allah, the Creator of the heavens and the earth. This awareness can transform Salah from a habitual routine into a profound spiritual experience.

The companions of the Prophet ﷺ understood this concept well. For instance, Ali ibn Abi Talib, the fourth caliph, was known for his deep concentration during prayer. It is reported that once an arrow was lodged in his body, and he requested that it be removed while he was in Salah, as he knew that he would be so absorbed in his prayer that he would not feel the pain. Such was the level of Khushu that the early Muslims achieved, where their connection with Allah in Salah was so strong that it eclipsed their physical pain and worldly concerns.

Khushu is closely linked to the understanding of what is being recited in Salah. The words of the Qur'an, which form the foundation of Salah, are not mere utterances but the direct speech of Allah. When a believer understands the meaning behind these words, it significantly enhances their experience of Salah. For instance, when reciting Surah Al-Fatihah, one is not just reading a text but is engaging in a conversation with Allah. Every phrase of the Surah has profound meaning, from praising Allah as the Lord of all the worlds to seeking His guidance on the straight path.

Understanding the Qur'an and its meanings can help a person attain a deeper sense of Khushu in Salah. When one contemplates the verses they recite, they become more connected to the essence of worship. For instance, when reciting *"Maliki Yawmid-Deen"* (Master of the Day of Judgment), a person is reminded of the Day of Judgment, when all of humanity will stand before Allah for accountability. This reflection instills a sense of fear and hope, drawing the worshipper closer to Allah.

The Prophet ﷺ exemplified how deeply understanding the Qur'an during prayer can move a person. There are numerous narrations of the Prophet weeping in prayer while reciting verses of the Qur'an. His Khushu was so profound that the words of Allah had a direct impact on his emotions and heart. In one instance, it is reported that during the night prayer (Tahajjud), the Prophet ﷺ stood for long hours reciting a single verse of the Qur'an while tears streamed down his face. The verse was: *"If You punish them, they are Your servants; but if You forgive them, indeed it is You who is the Exalted in Might, the Wise."* (Qur'an 5:118).

This depth of reflection on the Qur'an is a crucial part of developing Khushu. When one takes time to reflect on the meanings of the Qur'an, especially in Salah, the heart becomes more inclined towards Allah. Salah, therefore, transforms from a physical act into an intimate dialogue with the Creator, where every word and movement is filled with meaning and purpose.

For many believers, one of the biggest challenges in achieving Khushu is dealing with distractions. The nature of the human mind is such that it tends to wander, especially during moments of stillness. During Salah, the mind may drift to thoughts about work, family, or personal concerns. Overcoming these distractions requires discipline and practice. The Prophet Muhammad ﷺ gave practical advice to help believers focus during prayer. He advised, for example, to seek refuge in Allah from the whispers of Shaytan before starting the prayer by saying, *"A'udhu billahi min ash-shaytan ir-rajim."* This simple act can help clear the mind and direct one's focus towards Allah.

In addition, the Prophet ﷺ taught that preparing for Salah with sincerity and mindfulness is crucial. This includes performing Wudhu (ablution) with care, finding a quiet place for prayer, and removing any objects that might cause distraction. By creating an environment conducive to concentration, a person can increase their chances of maintaining Khushu throughout Salah.

Another essential aspect of developing Khushu is cultivating a deep love for Allah. When a believer truly loves Allah, their prayer becomes an act of devotion rather than a duty. This love transforms the way one approaches Salah. Rather than seeing it as an obligation that must be fulfilled, it becomes a cherished opportunity to spend time in the presence of Allah. The companions of the Prophet ﷺ demonstrated this love in their prayers, often prolonging their Salah out of sheer joy in worshipping their Lord.

The Prophet Muhammad ﷺ himself expressed this love for Salah when he said, *"The coolness of my eyes is in the prayer."* (Ahmad). This statement reflects the deep emotional connection the Prophet ﷺ had with his prayers. For him, Salah was a refuge from the difficulties of life, a moment of solace and peace where he could communicate directly with Allah. Cultivating this love for Salah is key to achieving Khushu, as it shifts the focus from external distractions to the internal desire to connect with Allah.

It is important to note that Khushu is not something that is attained overnight. It requires consistent effort, patience, and practice. The companions of the Prophet ﷺ, despite their deep faith, also faced moments of distraction and lack of focus during prayer. However, they persisted in their efforts to perfect their Salah and enhance their Khushu. Umar ibn Al-Khattab, for example, was known for his intense concentration during prayer, but even he would sometimes struggle with maintaining focus. He once remarked, *"I prepare myself for prayer, and when I stand, I struggle with distractions, but*

I remind myself again and again of the greatness of the One I am standing before."

This statement reflects the reality that Khushu is a journey, not a destination. It requires constant renewal of intention and continuous effort to bring the heart and mind back to Allah. The key is to never give up, even when distractions arise, and to always strive to improve one's connection with Allah through Salah.

One of the practical methods that the scholars recommend for attaining Khushu is to pause briefly between the movements of Salah. Rather than rushing through the prayer, one should take a moment to reflect at each stage. For instance, when moving from Ruku (bowing) to Sujood (prostration), a person should pause and allow their heart to absorb the significance of the movement. Ruku represents humility before Allah, while Sujood is the ultimate expression of submission. By taking a brief pause, the worshipper can internalize the meaning of each movement, allowing it to resonate in their heart.

Another recommended practice is to vary the Surahs and verses recited during Salah. This keeps the prayer from becoming monotonous and encourages the worshipper to engage with different parts of the Qur'an. By reciting different verses, a person can reflect on the diverse themes of the Qur'an, from the greatness of Allah to the descriptions of the Hereafter, thus enriching their prayer experience.

In addition to the physical and mental aspects of Khushu, the spiritual dimension plays a critical role. The heart must be fully engaged in Salah, recognizing the greatness of Allah and feeling a sense of awe and reverence. This spiritual state is nurtured by constantly remembering Allah outside of prayer. When a person consistently engages in Dhikr (remembrance of Allah) throughout the day, their heart becomes more inclined to experience Khushu during Salah. The Prophet ﷺ mentioned, *"The comparison of the one who remembers Allah and the one who does not is like the living and the dead."* (Bukhari).

This hadith highlights the transformative power of Dhikr in keeping the heart spiritually alive. When the heart is alive with the remembrance of Allah, it is easier to attain Khushu in Salah. The believer's soul is more attuned to the presence of Allah, and their heart is filled with a sense of nearness to Him.

Attaining Khushu in Salah is a reflection of one's relationship with Allah. When the heart is filled with love, fear, and hope in Allah, it is easier to achieve this level of focus and humility in prayer. Scholars of Islam have emphasized that Salah is not only a physical act but a spiritual engagement between the servant and their Lord. It is through the understanding of Allah's greatness and our own insignificance that a person can reach the desired state of Khushu.

A key element in this journey is understanding that Salah serves as a direct means of communicating with Allah. Every word spoken in Salah, especially during the recitation of Surah Al-Fatihah, is a dialogue with Allah. The believer praises Allah, seeks His guidance, and expresses their reliance on Him. When these words are spoken with sincerity and understanding, they penetrate the heart and bring the worshiper closer to Allah. This realization alone can shift the perspective of Salah from being an obligation to a heartfelt, purposeful act of worship.

Khushu also involves the correct performance of the physical postures in Salah. Every action, whether it's bowing in Ruku or prostrating in Sujood, is a testament to the humility of the believer before their Creator. When one performs these actions with the awareness that they are in the presence of Allah, it becomes easier to internalize the meanings behind them. For instance, the act of Sujood, where the forehead touches the ground, is the most humble position a human can assume. It is the point where the believer is closest to Allah, as mentioned in the hadith, *"The closest a servant is to his Lord is when he is in prostration."* (Muslim).

This position should evoke a deep sense of reverence and submission. When the believer understands that they are at their lowest physically, but at their highest spiritually, Sujood transforms into a moment of intense closeness to Allah. Many scholars have advised that during Sujood, one should prolong their supplications, as it is a time when the heart is most connected to its Lord.

One common issue faced by many Muslims is the rushing through the motions of Salah without giving proper attention to each movement and recitation. This is a major obstacle in achieving Khushu. The Prophet ﷺ warned against such hastiness in prayer. He taught that each movement in Salah must be performed with calmness and tranquility. It is narrated that the Prophet ﷺ once saw a man praying quickly without maintaining proper posture in Ruku and Sujood. The Prophet ﷺ said to him, *"Go back and pray, for you have not prayed."* (Bukhari).

This hadith highlights the importance of performing Salah with deliberation. A prayer that lacks proper posture and attentiveness is not accepted, as it goes against the essence of Khushu. The scholars have mentioned that to achieve Khushu, one must perform each posture with stillness, giving time for the body and heart to be fully engaged in the act of worship.

To enhance the experience of Khushu in Salah, it is also essential to remember the ultimate purpose of this act of worship. Salah is not merely a ritual, but a means of purification for the soul. It is through Salah that the believer attains closeness to Allah and seeks forgiveness for their sins. In fact,

28

one of the primary purposes of Salah is to serve as a shield against immoral and sinful behavior. Allah mentions in the Qur'an, *"Indeed, prayer prohibits immorality and wrongdoing."* (29:45).

However, for Salah to fulfill this role, it must be performed with sincerity and devotion. A prayer that is rushed or devoid of meaning will not have the desired effect on a person's character or actions. Khushu ensures that Salah serves as a transformative experience, helping the believer to detach from worldly concerns and focus solely on their relationship with Allah. This, in turn, leads to a more righteous and upright life, as the individual becomes more conscious of their actions and strives to live in accordance with the teachings of Islam.

Lastly, it is important to understand that Khushu is not a static state but a dynamic one that can fluctuate depending on the individual's spiritual condition. There may be times when Khushu is easily attained, and other times when distractions seem overwhelming. The key is to remain consistent in striving for Khushu, regardless of the challenges faced. The Prophet ﷺ taught that consistency in worship is beloved to Allah, even if the act is small. He said, *"The most beloved of deeds to Allah are those that are consistent, even if small."* (Bukhari).

This principle applies to Salah as well. Even if a person struggles to maintain Khushu in every prayer, their continuous effort to improve is what matters most. Over time, with persistence and sincerity, Allah will grant them the ability to experience deeper levels of Khushu. The journey towards achieving Khushu is one that requires patience, dedication, and a sincere desire to connect with Allah.

4: COMMON MISTAKES IN SALAH

Many individuals strive to perfect their Salah, yet due to certain misunderstandings or habitual errors, their prayers might lack the depth and spiritual focus that is central to its purpose. Common mistakes in Salah are not limited to errors in movement or recitation, but often revolve around one's state of mind and heart. These mistakes can prevent a person from attaining Khushu, which is the focus, humility, and submission required in Salah.

One of the most prevalent mistakes is the failure to prepare mentally and spiritually before entering Salah. For many, Salah becomes a habitual act, performed quickly and without thought. The mind is preoccupied with the tasks of daily life, making it difficult to focus on the greatness of Allah and the purpose of the prayer. Such a hurried and distracted approach to Salah significantly diminishes its impact on the soul and life of the believer.

Additionally, many people rush through their prayers, focusing more on completing the Salah than on engaging deeply with each word and movement. This haste contradicts the essence of Khushu, as true humility requires taking time to reflect on the meaning of the verses recited and the movements performed. The Prophet Muhammad (PBUH) emphasized the importance of performing Salah with tranquility, instructing believers to ensure that their postures are carried out with calmness and peace.

Another mistake frequently observed is the lack of proper recitation. Many worshippers, due to habit or neglect, do not take the time to recite the verses of the Qur'an clearly and thoughtfully. Rushing through Surah Al-Fatihah or other selected verses can hinder the spiritual connection that comes from contemplating the meanings of the words being spoken. Without understanding or reflecting on what is being recited, Salah becomes a mere physical exercise rather than an act of worship that engages both the heart and the mind.

Similarly, not observing the proper length and stillness in Ruku (bowing) and Sujood (prostration) is another common shortfall. It has been noted in the Sunnah that each position of Salah is meant to be a moment of reflection, humility, and submission to Allah. Rushing through these postures without taking time to pause and reflect contradicts the purpose of Salah and diminishes the opportunity for closeness to Allah.

This rushing through movements also extends to the transition between positions in Salah. The Prophet Muhammad (PBUH) instructed that believers should move between the standing, bowing, and prostration positions with calmness and deliberation, ensuring that each posture is completed with serenity before transitioning to the next. A lack of stillness and rushing through these postures negates the tranquility and humility that Khushu demands.

A less obvious but equally detrimental mistake is allowing one's mind to wander during Salah. This is one of the most common challenges faced by worshippers. The mind becomes occupied with worldly concerns—work, family, or personal worries—distracting the individual from the purpose of Salah. This mental distraction takes away from the connection with Allah and prevents the development of Khushu.

Scholars have offered various methods to combat this distraction, including understanding the meanings of the verses being recited, focusing on the movements of the Salah, and being mindful of the fact that Allah is observing the worshipper. The Prophet Muhammad (PBUH) taught that a person should perform Salah as though they see Allah, and though they may not see Him, they should always be conscious that He sees them. This level of mindfulness helps to guard against the wandering of the mind during prayer.

Another important aspect that is often overlooked is the intention (Niyyah). While the physical act of Salah is critical, the intention behind it is just as important. Some worshippers may perform Salah out of routine or obligation, rather than out of sincere devotion and desire to please Allah. This lack of sincerity in the intention can render the prayer devoid of its spiritual benefits. It is essential to approach each Salah with a renewed sense of purpose and a sincere heart, ensuring that the Niyyah is directed toward seeking closeness to Allah and fulfilling one's obligation as a Muslim.

Physical errors also contribute to common mistakes in Salah. These include failing to maintain the correct posture during the prayer. For example, in Ruku, some people fail to align their backs properly, which is essential for the completeness of the prayer. Similarly, in Sujood, it is important that the forehead and nose both touch the ground, as this represents the ultimate act of submission to Allah. Failing to perform these actions correctly not only diminishes the outward form of the prayer but also impacts its inward spiritual essence.

There are also mistakes made during the sitting portion of Salah, particularly during the Tashahhud. The sitting should be performed with calmness and stillness, and the fingers should be positioned in accordance with the Sunnah. Many people rush through this part of the prayer, not realizing its importance. The Tashahhud is a moment of deep reflection where the believer testifies to the oneness of Allah and acknowledges the Prophethood of Muhammad (PBUH). Skipping over this moment hurriedly detracts from the opportunity to engage meaningfully with these powerful declarations.

It is important to remember that Salah is a comprehensive act of worship that involves the mind, body, and soul. One of the frequent mistakes is the overemphasis on the external aspects of Salah while neglecting the internal, spiritual elements. Some individuals are meticulous about their posture and recitation but fail to cultivate the necessary humility and focus within their hearts. True Khushu requires a balance between the outward and inward aspects of Salah. It is not enough to simply perform the actions correctly; one must also engage their heart and mind, reflecting on the greatness of Allah and the significance of the prayer.

The position of the gaze during Salah is also significant. Some people look around the room or at distractions around them, which detracts from their focus on the prayer. The correct practice is to keep the gaze fixed on the place of Sujood throughout the prayer, as this helps maintain concentration and serves as a reminder of the humility and submission required in Salah.

Furthermore, a common error is the neglect of proper attire during Salah. While Islam places emphasis on modesty and cleanliness, many people overlook the importance of dressing appropriately for prayer. Wearing tight, revealing, or inappropriate clothing during Salah not only detracts from the reverence of the prayer but also contradicts the principles of modesty and humility that Salah requires. The Prophet Muhammad (PBUH) taught that clothing should cover the Awrah (the parts of the body that must be covered in front of others) and that worshippers should present themselves in a clean and dignified manner before Allah.

By paying attention to these aspects of Salah—both internal and external—one can move closer to perfecting their prayer and achieving Khushu. While some of these mistakes may seem minor, they collectively impact the quality and acceptance of the prayer. Rectifying these errors is essential for those who seek to elevate their connection with Allah through Salah.

Ultimately, the perfection of Salah is a lifelong endeavor. It requires ongoing self-reflection and a commitment to improving both the external and internal aspects of the prayer. Regularly revisiting the Sunnah and the teachings of the Prophet (PBUH) can provide guidance on how to avoid common mistakes and enhance the overall experience of Salah. Continuous improvement in one's prayer is a sign of a sincere desire to draw closer to Allah and fulfill His commandments in the best manner possible.

The journey towards Khushu in Salah is not one that can be completed overnight, but rather a consistent effort that must be made over time. As one becomes more aware of the common mistakes in prayer and strives to correct them, the spiritual depth and meaning of Salah will become more apparent. This, in turn, brings the worshipper closer to the ultimate purpose of Salah, which is to worship Allah with sincerity, humility, and focus.

In addition to the internal and external aspects of Salah, there is a significant focus on the timing of the prayer itself. One of the most common mistakes observed is the delay of Salah beyond its designated time. Allah has made the five daily prayers obligatory at specific times, and maintaining these times is crucial for the proper observance of Salah. The Qur'an emphasizes that believers should be punctual and regular in their prayers:

"Indeed, prayer has been decreed upon the believers a decree of specified times" (Surah An-Nisa, 4:103).

Delaying Salah without a valid reason diminishes its significance. Some people habitually postpone their prayer until the very last moment or even miss it altogether, intending to "make it up" later. This shows a lack of seriousness and can lead to carelessness in fulfilling one of the most important obligations in Islam. Praying on time reflects a believer's commitment to Allah's command and a prioritization of worship over worldly distractions.

Punctuality in prayer is also a means of disciplining the self and establishing a rhythm of worship throughout the day. By praying at the appointed times, a believer continually renews their connection with Allah and maintains an awareness of their purpose in life. Furthermore, praying at the beginning of the time window for each Salah carries additional reward, as it demonstrates eagerness to fulfill Allah's command.

The Prophet Muhammad (PBUH) emphasized the importance of praying at the earliest opportunity, saying:

"The best of deeds is to offer Salah at its early time" (Sahih Bukhari).

Therefore, developing the habit of praying promptly is a key aspect of improving one's Salah. It also helps to foster discipline in other aspects of life, as punctuality in worship cultivates a sense of order and mindfulness in one's daily routine.

Another mistake related to the timing of Salah is the lack of preparation before the prayer time arrives. Many people rush into prayer without taking the necessary time to prepare their minds, bodies, and surroundings. This lack of preparation can result in a hasty, distracted prayer, where the person is more focused on external matters than the act of worship. Preparing for Salah includes making the intention, performing Wudu (ablution) properly, and ensuring a clean and quiet space for prayer. These preparatory steps help to create a mental and spiritual state of readiness, allowing the worshipper to approach Salah with focus and devotion.

The Prophet Muhammad (PBUH) taught his companions the importance of calmness and preparation for Salah. Once, he observed a man rushing to join the congregation and instructed him to walk calmly, saying:
"When you come to the prayer, do not come running. Walk calmly and join the prayer with tranquility" (Sahih Bukhari).

This advice is not only for those who are late to a congregational prayer but serves as a general reminder to approach Salah with peace and calmness. Rushing into prayer after hurriedly completing tasks or thinking about what comes next reduces the ability to concentrate and connect with Allah.

The state of the heart is of utmost importance during Salah. If a person's heart is preoccupied with worldly matters, their focus will be diverted, and they will be unable to fully engage in the prayer. This can lead to a superficial performance of the Salah, where the physical actions are carried out, but the spiritual connection is lacking. Achieving Khushu requires a state of mental and emotional preparation before the Salah begins. Taking a few moments to clear the mind and focus on the intention of worship helps to set the right tone for the prayer.

Maintaining a clean and tranquil environment for Salah is another aspect that is often overlooked. While the state of the heart and mind is crucial, the physical space in which a person prays also plays a role in fostering concentration and devotion. Many people pray in cluttered or noisy environments, which can easily distract from the prayer. It is recommended to create a space for Salah that is free from distractions, ensuring that the area is clean and conducive to peaceful worship.

The importance of cleanliness in the place of prayer is emphasized in both the Qur'an and Sunnah. The Prophet Muhammad (PBUH) instructed that the area where one prays should be free of impurities, and it should not contain anything that could divert the attention of the worshipper. A clean, simple, and quiet space allows the individual to focus entirely on their connection with Allah without being distracted by external factors.

For many people, one of the greatest sources of distraction during Salah is the presence of their mobile phones. While technology can be a great aid in various aspects of life, it can also be a significant barrier to concentration in worship. Notifications, messages, and even the mere presence of a phone can pull one's mind away from the prayer. It is highly advisable to turn off or silence any devices before beginning Salah to ensure that the focus remains solely on Allah.

Another physical aspect of Salah that often needs attention is the condition of the clothing worn during the prayer. While it is common knowledge that the Awrah must be covered, some people neglect the quality and cleanliness of the clothing they wear during Salah. Wearing tight or revealing clothing, even if technically covering the Awrah, can diminish the reverence of the prayer. It is important to dress modestly and appropriately when standing before Allah in Salah.

The Prophet Muhammad (PBUH) advised believers to wear their best clothing when coming to prayer, as it reflects a level of respect and honor for the act of worship. Dressing in a manner that is befitting the solemnity of Salah demonstrates a conscious awareness of the significance of the prayer and the One to whom it is directed.

Furthermore, the physical posture and appearance during Salah also reflect the state of the heart. A person who stands before Allah with humility and reverence will naturally adopt a posture that reflects submission. Standing upright, bowing properly in Ruku, and prostrating with full humility in Sujood are all physical manifestations of a believer's inner state. It is through this combination of internal humility and external reverence that Salah becomes a truly transformative act of worship.

One of the most subtle mistakes in Salah is a lack of gratitude. While Salah is primarily an act of worship, it is also an opportunity to express gratitude to Allah for His countless blessings. Many people perform Salah as a mere obligation, without reflecting on the immense privilege it is to stand before their Creator in prayer. Salah is not a burden, but a gift—a means through which believers can draw closer to Allah, seek His forgiveness, and express their thankfulness for all that He has provided.

Reflecting on the blessings of life, health, sustenance, and guidance during Salah can deepen one's connection to the prayer. Each movement in Salah can be seen as an expression of gratitude: standing in submission, bowing in humility, and prostrating in awe of Allah's greatness. Cultivating an attitude of thankfulness in Salah enhances its spiritual benefits and brings the worshipper closer to achieving true Khushu.

To enhance this sense of gratitude, it is beneficial to recall specific blessings during the moments of quiet reflection in Salah. For example, during Sujood, one can take a moment to thank Allah for personal blessings, such as good health or the guidance to perform Salah itself. By doing so, the prayer becomes more than just a series of actions—it becomes a conversation with Allah, a time to acknowledge His mercy and express sincere gratitude for His endless favors.

Gratitude in Salah also extends to being mindful of the ability to pray itself. Many people around the world face obstacles that prevent them from performing Salah regularly, whether due to illness, conflict, or other hardships. Being able to pray freely, in peace, and with sound health is a blessing that should never be taken for granted. Recognizing this privilege can inspire a deeper connection to the prayer and a greater sense of responsibility in performing it with sincerity and devotion.

It is through Salah that a believer can seek to strengthen their relationship with Allah. Salah serves as a reminder of a person's purpose in life and provides a framework for living a life that is pleasing to Allah. By correcting the mistakes commonly made in Salah—whether they are related to timing, posture, focus, or intention—one can transform their prayer into a profound act of worship that brings peace to the heart and clarity to the soul.

The opportunity to connect with Allah five times a day through Salah is a mercy and a means of continuous spiritual renewal. For the believer who seeks closeness to their Creator, Salah is not merely an obligation but a refuge—a place of solace, reflection, and communication with Allah.

Maintaining the focus and humility in Salah is often a challenge due to the distractions of daily life. These distractions may be external, such as noise or interruptions, or internal, like wandering thoughts. One way to mitigate these distractions is by reminding oneself of the significance of standing before Allah. Before beginning Salah, it can be helpful to consciously remind oneself of the greatness of Allah, the purpose of life, and the reality of the Hereafter. This internal preparation helps create an atmosphere of seriousness and concentration, which can carry through the entire prayer.

Furthermore, the Prophet Muhammad (PBUH) advised believers to pray as if it were their last prayer. This advice instills a sense of urgency and focus in the worshipper, reminding them that life is fleeting and that every Salah may be their final opportunity to stand before Allah in worship. Adopting this mindset helps to push away distractions and increases the level of Khushu in Salah.

Salah is also an opportunity to reflect on one's shortcomings and sins. The moments of stillness, particularly in Sujood, are ideal for making personal Du'a and seeking forgiveness from Allah. It is in these moments of humility, with one's forehead pressed to the ground, that the believer is closest to their Lord. As the Prophet Muhammad (PBUH) said:

"The closest a servant is to his Lord is when he is in Sujood." (Sahih Muslim)

During Sujood, the worshipper's physical posture reflects the ultimate submission to Allah. It is an act of humility that symbolizes the believer's recognition of Allah's greatness and their own dependency on His mercy. It is important to take time in Sujood, allowing the heart and mind to fully connect with the act of worship. The Prophet (PBUH) taught that in Sujood, a person should prolong their supplication and ask Allah for what they need, both in this world and the Hereafter.

The importance of Sujood is further emphasized by the fact that it is the position in which Shaytan is most humiliated. Shaytan's refusal to prostrate to Adam (PBUH) led to his expulsion from Paradise, and thus every time a believer performs Sujood, it is a reminder of the believer's obedience to Allah and their rejection of Shaytan's rebellion. It is in Sujood that the believer affirms their allegiance to Allah alone and their rejection of arrogance and pride.

The state of mind during Sujood is critical. Instead of rushing through this part of Salah, one should strive to focus on their need for Allah's mercy, guidance, and forgiveness. By making sincere Du'a in this position, the believer opens the door to spiritual growth and the rectification of their relationship with Allah.

As Salah progresses, it is important to maintain the same level of concentration and devotion that is present at the beginning of the prayer. Often, worshippers start Salah with focus, only to find their attention waning as the prayer continues. To counter this, it is beneficial to remain mindful of the meaning behind each movement and recitation throughout the prayer. Understanding the meaning of the verses of the Qur'an recited during Salah can enhance one's connection to the prayer, as each verse serves as a reminder of Allah's mercy, power, and guidance.

For example, when reciting Surah Al-Fatiha, one is reminded of Allah's attributes—His mercy, His role as the Sustainer of all creation, and His power on the Day of Judgment. The believer is also reminded of their dependence on Allah's guidance, as they pray:

"Guide us to the straight path, the path of those who have earned Your favor, not of those who have gone astray." (Surah Al-Fatiha, 1:6-7)

Reciting these verses with understanding and contemplation can transform Salah into a profound conversation with Allah, where the believer is not just performing rituals, but seeking guidance and expressing their complete reliance on their Creator.

Another critical aspect of Salah is the proper observance of the physical movements. Each movement in Salah—whether it is standing, bowing, prostrating, or sitting—has a symbolic meaning and should be performed with precision and care. When a person rushes through these movements or performs them without mindfulness, the prayer loses its spiritual depth.

Ruku (bowing) is an essential part of Salah, symbolizing the worshipper's recognition of Allah's majesty and authority. In Ruku, the believer bows before Allah, acknowledging His greatness and their own submission to His will. It is important to perform Ruku with calmness and stillness, ensuring that the body is in the correct position before moving on to the next part of the prayer.

After Ruku, the worshipper rises to stand again, reciting:

"Sami'a Allahu liman hamidah" (*Allah hears those who praise Him*), followed by: *"Rabbana lakal hamd"* (*Our Lord, to You belongs all praise*).

This moment is an opportunity to reflect on Allah's hearing of all prayers and His deserving of all praise. By standing upright and taking a brief pause, the believer gives time for these profound meanings to settle in the heart before moving on to Sujood.

The transition from Ruku to Sujood is one of the most significant parts of Salah. It is a reminder of the journey from submission to humility. While Ruku represents submission, Sujood represents the ultimate state of humility and surrender. The worshipper physically lowers themselves to the ground, placing their forehead on the earth, symbolizing complete dependence on Allah.

In Sujood, the believer should feel the weight of their submission to Allah. It is a time to let go of all pride, arrogance, and attachment to worldly concerns, focusing entirely on the greatness of Allah and the smallness of the self. This act of prostration is not just a physical movement, but a deep spiritual gesture of humility and devotion.

The Prophet (PBUH) emphasized the importance of Sujood by encouraging believers to prolong this position and to make abundant supplications during it. It is in Sujood that the believer is closest to Allah, and it is a time to ask for anything they need, both in this world and the Hereafter. By extending the time spent in Sujood, the believer deepens their connection with Allah and increases their chances of having their prayers answered.

As the prayer comes to a close, the worshipper sits in At-Tahiyyat, reciting the words of praise and blessings upon the Prophet Muhammad (PBUH) and his family. This sitting posture is another moment of calm and reflection, where the believer acknowledges the role of the Prophet in conveying the message of Islam and asks Allah to bless him and his Ummah.

The final act of the prayer is the Tasleem, where the worshipper turns their head to the right and left, saying:

"As-salamu alaykum wa rahmatullah" (*Peace and mercy of Allah be upon you*).

This greeting of peace marks the end of the prayer, but it also serves as a reminder that the believer's responsibility to maintain peace and good conduct continues beyond the Salah. The Tasleem is not just a mechanical end to the prayer; it is a message to the worshipper that they should leave the prayer with a sense of peace, ready to engage with the world in a manner that reflects the values and teachings of Islam.

By focusing on the meaning and purpose of each part of the prayer, from the opening Takbeer to the final Tasleem, the believer can transform their Salah from a mere obligation into a source of spiritual nourishment and growth. The goal is not just to fulfill the external requirements of the prayer but to internalize its teachings and allow it to shape one's character, actions, and relationship with Allah.

5: **THE CONSEQUENCES OF HEEDLESSNESS IN SALAH**

In the daily life of a believer, Salah (prayer) stands as the most significant act of worship that connects a person to Allah. However, the value of this connection is greatly diminished when the heart is heedless during the prayer. Heedlessness, or lack of Khushu (focus, humility, and presence of mind), strips the prayer of its true spiritual benefits. The Qur'an warns against this heedlessness, not only in terms of negligence in performing the prayer itself but also in the state of the heart while performing it. Allah says:

"So woe to those who pray, but are heedless of their prayer." (Surah Al-Ma'un, 107:4-5)

This verse does not address those who do not pray at all but rather those who, despite praying, are careless and inattentive in their prayer. They rush through it without understanding the words, without feeling the presence of Allah, and without appreciating the significance of each movement. This heedlessness, according to the scholars of Islam, is dangerous because it may lead a person to completely lose the benefits of Salah, both in this world and the Hereafter.

The heedless worshipper may perform the physical actions of Salah correctly, but their heart remains distracted, thinking about worldly affairs, upcoming tasks, or even personal troubles. While this is a common issue, it is not one that should be accepted or allowed to persist. The Qur'an and Sunnah emphasize the need for both internal and external aspects of Salah to be aligned. The physical movements must reflect the humility of the heart, and the heart must remain focused on the worship of Allah alone.

One of the consequences of this heedlessness is that it renders the prayer ineffective as a tool for personal development. Salah, when performed with Khushu, serves as a constant reminder of the believer's purpose in life and keeps them away from sinful actions. As Allah states in the Qur'an:

"Indeed, prayer prohibits immorality and wrongdoing." (Surah Al-Ankabut, 29:45)

When Khushu is absent, however, this powerful effect of Salah is lost, and the person may continue to engage in sinful behavior, without feeling the guilt or responsibility that comes with neglecting one's connection to Allah.

The scholars have warned that a lack of Khushu in Salah can lead to hypocrisy. The hypocrites are described in the Qur'an as those who pray outwardly but lack sincerity in their hearts. They pray only to be seen by others and are negligent in their prayer. Allah says about the hypocrites:

"Indeed, the hypocrites seek to deceive Allah, but He is deceiving them. And when they stand for prayer, they stand lazily, showing themselves to the people and not remembering Allah except a little." (Surah An-Nisa, 4:142)

This verse is a reminder that a prayer devoid of sincerity, focus, and humility can lead to a dangerous spiritual state. While it may not be intentional, the heedless prayer can erode one's faith over time, distancing the believer from Allah's mercy.

Another consequence of heedlessness in Salah is the loss of its protective power. Salah, when performed with Khushu, acts as a shield against Shaytan and his whispers. It protects the heart from becoming attached to worldly desires and distractions. But when a person is heedless, Shaytan finds it easier to distract them, even within the prayer itself. He may cause their mind to wander, making them forget how many units (rak'ahs) they have prayed, or filling their thoughts with concerns unrelated to their worship.

The Prophet Muhammad (PBUH) said:

"When the call to prayer is made, Shaytan flees on his heels... But when the call is finished, Shaytan returns, until he comes between the man and his soul and says: Remember such and such a thing, remember such and such a thing, which he had not remembered, until the man does not know how many units he has prayed." (Sahih al-Bukhari)

This shows how Shaytan uses distractions as a tool to diminish the spiritual value of Salah. The more a person allows their mind to wander during prayer, the less effective it becomes in strengthening their relationship with Allah.

The heedlessness in prayer is not limited to distractions during the actual prayer time. It also includes procrastination or delaying the prayer until the last possible moment. This carelessness reflects a lack of priority given to the worship of Allah. The believer is expected to pray on time, recognizing that the Salah is a conversation with Allah and a way to honor Him. The Prophet (PBUH) taught that one of the most beloved deeds to Allah is prayer performed at its proper time.

The scholars have also warned that delaying prayer without valid reasons leads to a loss of blessings. Praying as soon as the time for Salah enters allows the believer to fully dedicate their heart and mind to worship without the stress of rushing through the prayer to meet a deadline. Delaying prayer until the last moment can result in hurried movements and a lack of concentration, further increasing the likelihood of heedlessness.

The consequences of heedlessness in Salah extend beyond this world. The Prophet Muhammad (PBUH) mentioned that on the Day of Judgment, the first action for which a person will be held accountable is their Salah. If the Salah is found to be deficient, it will affect the outcome of the entire reckoning. He said:

"The first thing for which the people will be called to account on the Day of Resurrection will be their prayers. Our Lord will say to His angels (although He knows best): Look at My servant's prayers, are they complete or incomplete? If they are complete, it will be written as complete. If they are incomplete, He will say: Look and see if My servant has any voluntary prayers. If he has them, He will say: Complete his obligatory prayers with his voluntary prayers. Then the rest of his deeds will be examined in the same way." (Sunan Abu Dawood)

This hadith emphasizes the gravity of Salah in determining a person's ultimate fate. Heedlessness in Salah, whether through lack of focus or consistent delay, jeopardizes the reward of the prayer and, by extension, the success of the believer in the Hereafter.

While the consequences of heedlessness in Salah are serious, they are not irreversible. Allah, in His infinite mercy, has given believers the opportunity to correct their mistakes and improve their prayer. It starts with making a firm intention to improve one's Khushu and taking practical steps toward achieving it. One of the first steps is to consciously remind oneself of the importance of Salah before every prayer. This can be done by reflecting on verses of the Qur'an and hadith that emphasize its value, as well as remembering that each prayer is an opportunity to draw closer to Allah.

The Prophet Muhammad (PBUH) also encouraged believers to pray as if it were their last prayer, saying:

"Pray as if you see Allah, and if you do not see Him, know that He sees you." (Sahih al-Bukhari)

This mindset helps create a sense of urgency and reverence in the heart, making it easier to focus and maintain Khushu throughout the prayer.

Another way to combat heedlessness is by understanding the meaning of what is being recited in Salah. Many believers memorize Surah Al-Fatiha and other short surahs from the Qur'an but may not fully comprehend the profound meanings behind the words. Taking the time to study the meaning and Tafsir of these surahs can significantly enhance the level of focus during Salah. When a person understands the words they are reciting, it becomes a conversation between the worshipper and Allah, making it easier to remain attentive.

Additionally, slowing down the pace of recitation and pausing to reflect after each verse can deepen the connection to the prayer. Rushing through the words or treating the recitation as a mechanical process robs the prayer of its spiritual depth. Instead, each verse should be recited with care, allowing the heart to absorb its message and turn toward Allah in sincerity.

Physical stillness in Salah is also crucial for maintaining Khushu. The Prophet (PBUH) warned against unnecessary movements and hastiness in Salah, as it detracts from the focus and humility required for a meaningful prayer. In one hadith, the Prophet (PBUH) described the prayer of someone who rushed through it without observing the proper pauses as invalid, advising them to repeat the prayer correctly.

By slowing down and performing each movement of Salah with deliberation and respect, the worshipper creates a sense of calmness that allows the heart to settle and focus on the worship of Allah. The movements in Salah, from standing to bowing, prostrating, and sitting, are not just physical acts but are deeply symbolic of the believer's submission and humility before Allah. Rushing through them undermines their significance.

The final step in combating heedlessness is to make Du'a regularly for improvement in Salah. Just as a person asks Allah for success in worldly matters, they should ask for success in their worship. The Prophet Muhammad (PBUH) frequently made Du'a for steadfastness in prayer, as recorded in this Du'a:

"O Allah, help me to remember You, to thank You, and to worship You in the best manner." (Sunan an-Nasa'i)

By turning to Allah and asking for assistance, the believer acknowledges their dependence on Him and seeks His guidance in improving their Salah. This reliance on Allah fosters a deeper connection and a greater sense of humility during the prayer.

In addition to making Du'a, creating an environment conducive to concentration can help a person stay focused during Salah. For example, choosing a quiet, clean, and distraction-free place for prayer can make a significant difference. The Prophet (PBUH) preferred to pray in an environment that allowed for complete focus and would encourage others to do the same. Praying in a space where one feels at peace, away from noise or interruptions, is one of the key elements to achieving Khushu.

For those who live in busy environments or have families, it may be helpful to plan for Salah at a time when the household is calm. This could be early in the morning, late at night, or during moments when everyone is engaged in other activities. Additionally, turning off electronic devices and setting aside other distractions can greatly improve the quality of the prayer. The goal is to create a mental and physical space where the mind can focus entirely on the remembrance of Allah.

Developing the habit of being mindful before Salah also plays a crucial role in achieving Khushu. One of the main reasons people are distracted during prayer is that they rush into it without proper mental preparation. Taking a few moments before starting Salah to gather one's thoughts and focus on the upcoming conversation with Allah can significantly enhance the level of concentration.

The Prophet Muhammad (PBUH) taught the importance of approaching prayer with a calm and reflective attitude. He encouraged his companions to perform their Wudu (ablution) with care and to enter into Salah with a sense of awe for the significance of what they were about to do. This mindfulness before the prayer begins allows the worshipper to mentally detach from worldly concerns and immerse themselves in the act of worship.

In some cases, physical health can also affect one's ability to focus during Salah. If a person is hungry, tired, or unwell, their mind may struggle to concentrate. Islam emphasizes the importance of physical well-being and how it impacts worship. The Prophet (PBUH) would advise his companions to avoid praying when they were hungry or fatigued because these physical needs can prevent the heart and mind from engaging in the prayer fully.

If a person finds it difficult to concentrate due to such reasons, they should take steps to address their physical needs before prayer. This could mean eating a light meal before Salah, getting adequate rest, or addressing any medical concerns that might affect focus. By ensuring the body is well-rested and nourished, the worshipper can approach Salah with greater energy and attention, enhancing their experience.

As a believer strives to improve their Salah, they should remain patient and persistent in their efforts. Achieving perfect Khushu in every prayer is a lifelong goal, and no one is free from occasional distractions. Even the most pious individuals experience moments of wandering thoughts during Salah. However, what distinguishes a mindful worshipper is their willingness to consistently bring their attention back to Allah whenever they find their mind drifting.

One of the most effective ways to develop this skill is through regular practice and self-awareness. The more a person consciously works to improve their focus in Salah, the more they will notice when distractions arise. When a distracting thought enters the mind, it's important to gently push it aside and refocus on the words being recited and the actions being performed. Over time, this discipline strengthens the ability to maintain Khushu for longer periods.

The reward for improving one's Salah is not limited to the Hereafter. A prayer performed with Khushu has immediate benefits in the life of the believer. It brings a sense of peace and contentment that carries over into other aspects of life. The Prophet Muhammad (PBUH) described Salah as a means of relieving stress and anxiety, saying:

"O Bilal, give us rest with it (the prayer)." (Sunan Abi Dawood)

This statement highlights the therapeutic nature of Salah when performed with sincerity and focus. It is not just a religious duty but a refuge for the believer, offering moments of stillness and calm amidst the chaos of daily life. By making Salah a priority and striving to perform it with full attention, a person can experience its power as a source of emotional and spiritual healing.

It is also important to remember that Salah is a private conversation between the worshipper and Allah. This intimate nature of Salah should encourage the believer to be sincere in their efforts to improve their prayer. Unlike other acts of worship, such as charity or fasting, Salah is performed alone, without the need for external validation. Its benefits are deeply personal, and its rewards are known only to Allah.

The private nature of Salah serves as a reminder that it is an act of love and devotion, meant to strengthen the relationship between the believer and their Creator. The more sincere a person is in their prayer, the more they will feel the closeness of Allah and experience the peace that comes with it. This sincerity can only be achieved through a genuine desire to please Allah and a commitment to improving the quality of the prayer.

The significance of sincerity (Ikhlas) in Salah cannot be overstated. Many scholars emphasize that the outward actions of Salah, while important, are secondary to the inner state of the heart. A person may perform all the physical actions of Salah perfectly, but if their heart is not engaged in worship, the prayer lacks its true essence. Sincerity is what transforms the prayer from a mere physical routine into a profound act of worship that connects the believer to Allah.

To cultivate sincerity, the worshipper must constantly remind themselves of the purpose of Salah. It is not just an obligation but an opportunity to draw closer to Allah and seek His guidance and forgiveness. Each time a person stands in prayer, they should reflect on the greatness of Allah and the immense blessing it is to be able to speak directly to Him. This awareness of Allah's presence helps develop a deeper sense of sincerity and devotion in the heart.

One of the most powerful ways to increase sincerity in Salah is by reflecting on the words being recited, especially Surah Al-Fatiha. This chapter of the Qur'an is recited in every unit of Salah and is considered a dialogue between the worshipper and Allah. When a person understands that each verse is a direct conversation with Allah, it helps to increase their concentration and sincerity.

For example, when the believer says, *"Praise be to Allah, the Lord of all the worlds,"* they are acknowledging the greatness and majesty of Allah. When they say, *"You alone we worship, and You alone we ask for help,"* they are renewing their commitment to worship Allah sincerely and to rely on Him for all their needs. Reflecting on these meanings during Salah enhances the experience and helps prevent the heart from becoming heedless.

In addition to sincerity, humility (Tawadu') is another essential quality for a meaningful Salah. The act of bowing and prostrating before Allah is a physical manifestation of the humility that should be present in the heart. Salah is a reminder of the believer's dependence on Allah and their need for His mercy and guidance. Each movement in the prayer, from the standing posture to the prostration, symbolizes the believer's submission and obedience to their Creator.

Humility in Salah also requires a recognition of one's own shortcomings and sins. The believer should approach each prayer with a sense of humility, acknowledging their need for Allah's forgiveness and striving to improve their relationship with Him. This mindset helps to purify the heart and enhances the spiritual benefits of Salah, making it a source of true guidance and strength.

To maintain humility and sincerity in Salah, it is essential to avoid arrogance or complacency. Even if a person has prayed for many years, they should never feel that they have mastered Salah or that their prayer is perfect. There is always room for improvement, and every believer should strive to perfect their prayer throughout their lifetime. The companions of the Prophet (PBUH) were known for their constant efforts to improve their Salah, and they would often weep in prayer, reflecting on their need for Allah's mercy.

The pursuit of excellence in Salah is a journey that continues throughout one's life. It requires patience, dedication, and a willingness to learn and grow. By taking practical steps to improve Khushu, sincerity, and humility in Salah, the believer strengthens their connection to Allah and experiences the profound peace and contentment that comes from worshiping Him with a sincere heart.

6: **PRACTICAL STEPS TO DEVELOP KHUSHU**

Khushu, or mindfulness in Salah, is a quality that every believer should strive for, as it brings one closer to Allah and elevates the spiritual value of the prayer. Achieving Khushu is not an overnight process but requires dedication, patience, and consistent effort. One of the primary steps in developing Khushu is to begin by understanding the weight and importance of Salah in one's life. This realization itself motivates a person to give their full attention to their prayer and to make it meaningful.

Start by preparing mentally before the prayer. One of the best ways to prepare is to take a few moments before starting Salah to clear the mind of worldly distractions. This could involve reflecting on the greatness of Allah, the temporary nature of the world, and the purpose of worship. When a person steps into the prayer with their heart inclined towards Allah, they are more likely to maintain focus throughout the prayer.

The Prophet Muhammad (PBUH) taught his companions to perfect their Wudu, as it is the first step towards attaining Khushu. Performing Wudu with mindfulness and concentration helps the believer cleanse themselves both physically and spiritually, setting the tone for an attentive Salah. When making ablution, remember that it is not just about washing the limbs; it is an act of purification that removes sins. Reflecting on this helps to cultivate an attitude of humility and reverence before starting the prayer.

Additionally, choosing the right environment for Salah is crucial. Distractions can easily divert one's attention away from the prayer, so finding a quiet and clean place, free of disturbances, aids in focusing on the conversation with Allah. The Prophet (PBUH) would often seek out calm and serene places for prayer, and this practice encourages the believer to create a space where their heart can connect to Allah without interruptions.

Another important step in developing Khushu is understanding the meaning of the words being recited in Salah. Often, the lack of concentration stems from not fully comprehending the significance of what is being said. For those who do not understand Arabic, learning the meaning of Surah Al-Fatiha and the various supplications recited during prayer can make a profound difference. When a person knows what they are saying, they can engage their heart and mind in the prayer, rather than simply reciting the words.

Reflecting on the meaning of each verse brings the worshipper closer to Allah and enhances the sincerity of the prayer. For example, when reciting *"Alhamdulillahi Rabbil 'Aalamemeen,"* which translates to *"All praise is due to Allah, the Lord of all worlds,"* the believer should contemplate the countless blessings of Allah in their life and the vastness of His creation. This reflection nurtures a sense of gratitude and awe, which naturally enhances Khushu. Similarly, when reciting *"Maliki Yawmid-Deen,"* or *"Master of the Day of Judgment,"* one should remind themselves of the Day of Judgment and the accountability that awaits every soul. This deepens one's sense of responsibility and humility before Allah.

The physical aspects of Salah also play a role in cultivating Khushu. The positions of standing, bowing, and prostrating are not mere rituals but expressions of submission and servitude to Allah. When bowing in Ruku, for instance, reflect on the act of humbling oneself before the Creator. During Sujood, remember that this is the closest a servant comes to Allah. This consciousness in the body's movements aligns with the heart's devotion, strengthening the believer's focus and sincerity.

Another key element in achieving Khushu is patience. It is natural for the mind to wander, especially in the beginning stages of working on concentration. However, what distinguishes a person striving for Khushu is their ability to gently bring their mind back to focus whenever it drifts. This practice of refocusing the mind during prayer is an act of worship itself, showing one's dedication to perfecting their Salah.

The Prophet Muhammad (PBUH) advised the companions to avoid haste in their prayer, as rushing through it diminishes the quality of Khushu. Performing each movement with deliberation, whether it is Ruku, Sujood, or even the recitation, is vital. By slowing down and taking time in each posture, a person can internalize the significance of each action, allowing their heart to connect more deeply with Allah.

The Sunnah teaches us to pray as if we can see Allah, and if not, to remember that He sees us. This mindset, known as *Ihsan*, is one of the highest levels of faith and significantly impacts the quality of Khushu. When a person internalizes that they are standing before their Creator, the sense of awe and reverence naturally intensifies. This realization encourages the believer to approach the prayer with sincerity, humility, and mindfulness, knowing that they are in direct communication with the One who created them.

Incorporating this mindfulness into daily prayers requires practice, but over time, it becomes a natural part of the prayer routine. It is important to constantly remind oneself that the prayer is not just a ritual, but an opportunity to converse with Allah, seek His guidance, and express gratitude and humility before Him.

It is also essential to safeguard oneself from distractions that may arise during the prayer. Distractions are often internal, such as thoughts about worldly matters, but they can also be external, like noise or interruptions. To avoid these, a person can adopt practices such as praying in a quiet place, turning off any devices that may cause disturbance, and clearing the mind before starting the prayer.

The Prophet (PBUH) emphasized the importance of controlling distractions by saying, *"When the call to prayer is made, Satan flees with great speed."* Therefore, it is advisable to minimize sources of distraction, allowing the heart to be fully present. To further support this, a believer should make a habit of seeking refuge from Satan, saying *"A'udhu Billahi Minash Shaytanir Rajim,"* which protects the prayer from being corrupted by wandering thoughts.

A common obstacle to achieving Khushu is becoming overly focused on the mechanical aspects of the prayer, such as perfecting the movements and the pronunciation of words, while neglecting the spiritual connection to Allah. While it is essential to pray correctly, the outward actions should not take precedence over the inner experience of connecting with Allah. True Khushu comes when both the outward and inward aspects of the prayer are in harmony.

Maintaining the balance between the physical and spiritual aspects of the prayer is an ongoing process. The heart must be trained to remain present during the prayer, and the believer must strive to align their inner state with their external actions. The prayer should not be seen as a mere checklist of rituals but as a sacred moment of engagement with the Lord of the worlds.

Reflecting on the temporary nature of this world and the permanence of the hereafter is a powerful motivator for attaining Khushu. The Prophet Muhammad (PBUH) would often remind the companions of the fleeting nature of this life, and this perspective encouraged them to invest their hearts in worship. A believer should remind themselves during prayer that this world is transient, and only the relationship with Allah remains. This focus helps divert the heart from worldly concerns and brings clarity of purpose to the prayer.

Remembering death during prayer is another means of cultivating Khushu. The Prophet (PBUH) advised believers to pray as if it were their last prayer.

This mindset instills a sense of urgency and importance in the prayer, making it less likely for the worshipper to become distracted. When a person prays with the awareness that this could be their final moment of connection with Allah, they are more likely to be sincere and attentive in their prayer.

It is also crucial to maintain a level of humility and humbleness in prayer. Pride and arrogance are the enemies of Khushu, as they distance the heart from Allah. A humble heart recognizes its neediness before the Creator and approaches the prayer with an attitude of gratitude and reliance on Allah's mercy. The believer must constantly remind themselves that they are servants of Allah, standing before Him in complete submission and humility.

The example of the Prophet Muhammad (PBUH) demonstrates the importance of humility in prayer. He would often shed tears during prayer, overwhelmed by the awareness of Allah's greatness and the weight of the responsibility of worship. This profound humility serves as a model for believers to emulate, encouraging them to approach the prayer with a softened heart and a sincere desire to connect with Allah.

The companions of the Prophet (PBUH) also exemplified this level of humility in prayer. Abu Bakr (RA) was known to weep during his recitation of the Quran, deeply moved by the words of Allah. This emotional connection with the prayer is a reflection of a heart that is fully engaged and mindful of its purpose. Similarly, Umar ibn Al-Khattab (RA), despite his strength and authority, would cry in Salah, particularly when reflecting on verses of the Quran that reminded him of his own accountability before Allah.

This deep emotional connection with prayer is not a sign of weakness but of spiritual maturity. When a person is moved by the words of Allah, it shows that their heart is alive with faith and humility. Every believer should aspire to develop this level of connection in their prayers, as it signifies a true bond with their Creator.

In addition to humility, consistency in prayer is vital for nurturing Khushu. It is not enough to pray mindfully on occasion; rather, one must strive for consistency in their focus and devotion. Allah loves those acts of worship that are small but consistent. This means that even if a person struggles with maintaining concentration in every prayer, their continuous effort and dedication are what count in the eyes of Allah.

Praying the voluntary Sunnah prayers helps build this consistency. The Prophet (PBUH) emphasized the importance of these additional prayers as they complement the obligatory ones and help the believer draw closer to Allah. Over time, these voluntary prayers can serve as a training ground for developing Khushu, as they allow the worshipper to practice mindfulness and focus outside the mandatory prayers.

Furthermore, reflecting on the rewards promised by Allah for those who pray with Khushu is another powerful motivator. The Quran speaks of the success of those who are humble in their prayers, stating, *"Certainly will the believers have succeeded: They who are during their prayer humbly submissive."* This success is not just limited to the hereafter but extends to a sense of peace and tranquility in this life. When a person prays with Khushu, they find inner peace, knowing that they are fulfilling their purpose and drawing closer to Allah.

The promise of success for those who maintain Khushu in their prayers serves as a reminder of the ultimate goal of life: to please Allah and attain His mercy. This awareness encourages the believer to put forth their best effort in each prayer, knowing that it is a means of securing success in both this world and the hereafter.

Achieving Khushu is not limited to the actual moments of prayer. The believer's behavior outside of Salah also impacts their ability to focus and connect during the prayer. A person who lives their life in accordance with the commands of Allah, who engages in regular remembrance of Him, and who strives to purify their heart from sins will naturally find it easier to maintain Khushu during Salah. Conversely, a person who is negligent in their duties to Allah outside of prayer will struggle to find focus and sincerity in their worship.

Maintaining good character, avoiding sinful behavior, and being mindful of one's actions throughout the day help to create an environment in which Khushu can flourish. The heart that is constantly engaged in the remembrance of Allah outside of prayer is more likely to remain focused and connected during the prayer itself.

Patience is also essential when striving for Khushu. Developing mindfulness and concentration in Salah is a gradual process, and it is normal to face challenges along the way. However, it is important to remain committed to the goal and not become discouraged by setbacks. The effort to focus, even if imperfect, is valuable in the sight of Allah, and with time, the ability to maintain Khushu will improve.

The believer must remind themselves that Salah is a journey, and each prayer is an opportunity to grow closer to Allah. The struggles faced in developing Khushu are part of that journey, and they are a test of one's sincerity and dedication. By remaining patient and persevering through challenges, a person can ultimately achieve the peace and tranquility that come with Khushu.

Another important aspect of cultivating Khushu is being mindful of the words recited during the prayer. Understanding the meaning behind the verses of the Quran and the supplications recited enhances the spiritual experience.

When a person knows the significance of each phrase, it becomes easier to focus, and the heart naturally connects with the words being spoken. For example, when saying *"Subhana Rabbiyal 'Adheem"* in Ruku (bowing), one should reflect on the greatness of Allah, glorifying Him with full awareness of His majesty and power.

This mindfulness transforms the prayer from a series of ritualistic movements into an intimate conversation with Allah. It is a form of spiritual discipline that elevates the entire act of worship. Additionally, understanding the deeper meanings of verses such as *"Iyyaka Na'budu wa Iyyaka Nasta'een"* (You alone we worship, and You alone we ask for help) instills a sense of reliance and humility. It becomes a direct plea to Allah for guidance and support, reinforcing the believer's dependence on Him in all matters of life.

The Prophet Muhammad (PBUH) encouraged his companions to memorize and understand the meanings of various supplications. Doing so aids in achieving Khushu, as the heart and mind are engaged in the prayer. When the worshipper reflects on the power of the words they recite, their emotional connection to the prayer deepens. The simple act of saying *"Allahu Akbar"* at the beginning of each movement can serve as a reminder of Allah's greatness, helping to bring the heart back to focus if it begins to stray.

Incorporating reflection on the meanings of supplications and Quranic verses is a practice that can be developed over time. One practical way to achieve this is by taking the time outside of prayer to study the meanings and significance of the words. As the believer becomes more familiar with what they are reciting, their focus and connection during the prayer will naturally increase.

Moreover, making du'a (supplication) at the appropriate moments during prayer is another way to maintain focus and sincerity. The times of Sujood and before Tasleem (ending the prayer) are ideal moments for making personal supplications to Allah. During Sujood, the heart is in a state of complete humility, and the believer is closest to their Creator. It is during this time that one can pour out their concerns, express their hopes, and seek Allah's guidance in all aspects of life.

The Prophet Muhammad (PBUH) said, *"The closest that a servant is to his Lord is while he is in Sujood, so make plenty of du'a."* This demonstrates the importance of seizing the opportunity during prayer to connect with Allah on a deeper level. Making heartfelt du'a not only strengthens the individual's connection with Allah but also reinforces the mindfulness and sincerity that are essential to achieving Khushu.

Consistency in seeking forgiveness and repenting for sins also plays a crucial role in achieving Khushu. The believer who constantly turns to Allah in repentance clears their heart of the burdens of sin, making it easier to maintain focus and humility in prayer. A heart weighed down by sins is more prone to distractions and negligence in Salah. On the other hand, a heart that regularly seeks Allah's forgiveness is more open to experiencing the tranquility that comes with Khushu.

It is a practice of the righteous to ask for forgiveness at various points throughout the day, and especially during prayer. The act of asking for forgiveness, both before and after the prayer, helps to purify the heart and prepare it for sincere worship. As the Prophet (PBUH) taught, *"O people, turn to Allah in repentance and seek His forgiveness, for I turn to Him in repentance one hundred times a day."* This consistent habit of seeking forgiveness ensures that the heart remains soft, receptive, and ready to engage in sincere prayer.

Lastly, surrounding oneself with an environment conducive to mindfulness is crucial for maintaining Khushu. This involves not only choosing a quiet, distraction-free place to pray but also cultivating a lifestyle that fosters spirituality. The Prophet Muhammad (PBUH) often sought solitude for reflection and prayer, and this practice is encouraged for those seeking to deepen their connection with Allah. Eliminating distractions, whether physical or mental, sets the stage for a more meaningful and focused prayer.

Living a life that is centered around the remembrance of Allah throughout the day—whether through regular Quran recitation, dhikr (remembrance), or du'a—fosters a state of constant mindfulness. This mindfulness carries over into the prayer, making it easier to maintain focus and sincerity. When a person's entire lifestyle is built on the foundations of faith, Khushu in prayer becomes a natural extension of their devotion to Allah.

By committing to a lifestyle of spiritual discipline, regularly seeking forgiveness, and being mindful of both the external and internal aspects of Salah, the believer can achieve the true essence of Khushu and elevate their prayer to the level that brings peace, contentment, and success in both this world and the hereafter.

7: PHYSICAL POSTURES AND THEIR ROLE IN KHUSHU

The physical postures of Salah are not mere ritualistic actions; they serve a deeper purpose, bringing the body and heart into alignment with devotion. Each movement carries with it a symbolic and spiritual meaning, contributing to the state of Khushu. The most profound of these movements are the Ruku (bowing) and Sujood (prostration), both of which symbolize submission to Allah's will.

Ruku is the act of bowing, with the back and head aligned in a position of humility. It signifies the acknowledgment of Allah's greatness and the believer's readiness to submit to His commandments. This action serves as a reminder of our limited power and total dependence on Allah. When performed correctly, Ruku humbles the body, and the heart follows, leading the worshipper to a state of Khushu.

Sujood, the act of prostration, is the ultimate form of submission in Salah. It represents the lowest physical point a person can reach, with their forehead touching the ground, which serves as a profound reminder of human insignificance before the Creator. In this position, the believer acknowledges the greatness of Allah and their need for His mercy. This physical act of submission is accompanied by the glorification of Allah, as the worshipper says, *"Subhana Rabbiyal A'la"* (Glory be to my Lord, the Most High), reinforcing a deep sense of humility.

Beyond the symbolic meaning of each posture, the physical actions of Salah have a direct impact on the spiritual state of the believer. The body's movements are synchronized with the heart's intentions, and when this synchronization is achieved, it creates a profound sense of inner peace. This harmony between the physical and spiritual dimensions is essential for attaining Khushu. A heart that submits along with the body experiences the full power of Salah as a transformative act of worship.

The importance of performing each posture with precision cannot be overstated. Hastily performing these actions or neglecting their proper form diminishes the spiritual benefit of the prayer. For example, when one rushes through Ruku or Sujood without taking the time to fully submit and reflect on the greatness of Allah, the heart is deprived of the tranquility that comes with these actions. Each movement should be executed with calmness, ensuring that the body is fully at rest before transitioning to the next posture.

In addition, the posture of Qiyam (standing) before entering into Ruku is another crucial moment in Salah. This is the time when the worshipper stands in front of Allah, reciting His words from the Qur'an. The stillness and dignity of this posture reflect the seriousness of the interaction between the worshipper and their Creator. Standing straight with humility, hands folded, and eyes lowered toward the place of prostration, the believer prepares mentally and spiritually for the act of bowing.

Maintaining focus during Qiyam is essential for achieving Khushu in the following movements. The recitation of Qur'anic verses should not be mechanical, but rather filled with reflection and awe. Each verse recited is an opportunity to connect with Allah, to reflect on His words, and to internalize their meanings. For instance, when reciting *"Alhamdulillahi Rabbil 'Alameen"* (All praise is for Allah, Lord of all the worlds), the heart should acknowledge Allah's greatness and His provision for every creature. This level of consciousness strengthens the connection between the body's physical actions and the heart's submission, leading to Khushu.

The transition from Qiyam to Ruku should be slow and deliberate. Rushing through this movement breaks the flow of tranquility and prevents the heart from achieving a state of calm submission. Instead, as the worshipper moves from standing to bowing, they should focus on the act of leaving behind their worldly concerns, focusing entirely on Allah. It is in this moment that the body physically bends in acknowledgment of Allah's supreme authority, symbolizing the believer's submission.

In Ruku, the position of the body is important. The back should be straight, with the head aligned with the spine, representing balance and humility. The act of saying *"Subhana Rabbiyal 'Adheem"* (Glory be to my Lord, the Almighty) reinforces this submission, reminding the worshipper of Allah's power and majesty. This moment should be one of complete stillness and reflection, as the heart is humbled before Allah.

After Ruku, the worshipper stands up straight, saying *"Sami'Allahu liman hamidah"* (Allah hears those who praise Him). This transition from bowing to standing is significant. It represents the return to a state of readiness to receive Allah's mercy and to continue praising Him. The body once again aligns itself, and the heart remains focused on Allah's greatness. This moment of standing is one of gratitude, as the worshipper acknowledges Allah's constant hearing of their prayers and praises.

The next posture, Sujood, is the most intimate and profound expression of submission in Salah. In this position, the worshipper places their forehead on the ground, the lowest possible point, while glorifying Allah with *"Subhana Rabbiyal A'la"* (Glory be to my Lord, the Most High). The act of lowering oneself to the ground is symbolic of absolute surrender, as the worshipper acknowledges that they are nothing without Allah's mercy and guidance. Sujood is the closest a person can be to Allah during prayer, and it is a time when the heart is most open to supplication and reflection.

The stillness in Sujood is crucial. Rushing through this posture, or failing to rest in it, robs the believer of the opportunity to experience the deep spiritual connection that comes from true submission. Remaining in Sujood for a few moments, reflecting on the greatness of Allah, and making personal du'a allows the heart to soften and to truly connect with Allah.

The transition from Sujood to sitting is another moment of calm and reflection. The body rises from the ground, but the heart remains in a state of submission. This posture, known as Jalsah, is a moment of pause between two prostrations. The Prophet Muhammad (PBUH) encouraged his companions to sit in this posture with calmness, ensuring that the body was fully at rest before returning to Sujood. This moment of stillness allows the worshipper to reflect on the act of submission they just performed and to prepare themselves for the next prostration.

The second Sujood mirrors the first in its significance and depth. Once again, the worshipper lowers their body to the ground, placing their forehead on the earth in submission to Allah. This repetition of Sujood reinforces the humility and sincerity of the believer, as they continue to glorify Allah and seek His mercy. By taking time to reflect on the words being recited and the actions being performed, the believer deepens their state of Khushu, ensuring that their prayer is not merely a series of movements but a true act of worship.

Finally, the posture of Tashahhud, where the worshipper sits at the end of the prayer, is a moment of reflection and supplication. In this position, the believer recites the testimony of faith, declaring their belief in the oneness of Allah and the prophethood of Muhammad (PBUH). This declaration serves as a reminder of the purpose of life and the ultimate goal of worship—to live in accordance with Allah's will and to seek His pleasure.

The Tashahhud is a culmination of the worshipper's spiritual journey through Salah. Sitting in this posture, the worshipper reflects upon the core beliefs of Islam. By reciting *"Ashhadu alla ilaha illallah, wa ashhadu anna Muhammadan abduhu wa rasooluhu"* (I bear witness that there is no god but Allah, and I bear witness that Muhammad is His servant and messenger), the believer reaffirms their complete submission to Allah alone. It is a powerful moment of reconnection with one's faith, reminding the individual of their purpose and the transient nature of worldly life.

During the Tashahhud, the worshipper raises their right index finger as a symbol of Tawheed (the oneness of Allah). This small, but significant, gesture serves to focus the mind on the essence of Islamic belief—the singular worship of Allah. In this moment, the body remains still, but the heart is full of conviction, reinforcing the connection between outward physical action and inner spiritual awareness.

The Tashahhud is also a time for the worshipper to seek peace and blessings upon the Prophet Muhammad (PBUH) and his family. The recitation of *"Allahumma salli ala Muhammad wa ala aali Muhammad"* (O Allah, send Your peace and blessings upon Muhammad and his family) is a moment of gratitude and reverence, acknowledging the mercy that Allah bestowed upon the Prophet, and by extension, upon the entire Ummah. This part of the prayer is a powerful reminder of the interconnectedness of the Muslim community, transcending time and space.

After completing the Tashahhud, the worshipper turns their attention to the supplications that follow. These supplications are not mere formalities, but a sincere plea for protection and guidance. The believer asks Allah for refuge from the trials of life, the punishments of the grave, and the torments of the Fire. These du'as serve to remind the worshipper of their dependence on Allah for guidance and mercy, reinforcing the idea that without Allah's aid, they cannot hope to succeed in this life or the hereafter.

The final act of Salah is the Tasleem, where the worshipper turns their head to the right and then to the left, saying *"Assalamu Alaikum wa Rahmatullah"* (Peace and mercy of Allah be upon you). This action signifies the conclusion of the prayer, but it also carries a deeper meaning. The Tasleem is a declaration of peace, not only upon those present but also upon the angels who record deeds and the larger community of believers. It is a symbolic end to the prayer, transitioning the worshipper back into the world, but with a renewed sense of peace, purpose, and submission to Allah.

Even though the Tasleem marks the physical end of Salah, the effects of the prayer linger. A prayer performed with Khushu continues to influence the heart and mind long after the worshipper has said the final *"Assalamu Alaikum"*. This is the true measure of a successful Salah—its ability to transform the worshipper's character and actions outside the prayer.

Salah, when performed with sincerity and humility, acts as a shield against immoral behavior. Allah promises in the Qur'an, *"Indeed, prayer prohibits immorality and wrongdoing"* (29:45). This promise is actualized when the worshipper's heart is fully engaged in the prayer, absorbing the spiritual lessons embedded in each movement and recitation. Salah becomes more than just a ritual; it becomes a transformative experience that helps the believer maintain righteousness in every aspect of life.

The physical postures of Salah, when combined with the proper mindset, create a holistic act of worship that touches every part of the believer's life. Ruku, Sujood, and the other movements of prayer are not isolated actions, but rather steps on a journey toward spiritual refinement. Each posture humbles the body, and in turn, the heart. This humility carries over into the rest of the believer's life, fostering qualities such as patience, compassion, and gratitude.

The importance of the physical aspects of Salah is further emphasized by the hadith in which the Prophet Muhammad (PBUH) said, *"Pray as you have seen me praying"* (Bukhari). This command to emulate the Prophet's way of prayer is a reminder that every aspect of Salah—from the words recited to the way we stand, bow, and prostrate—should be performed with care and mindfulness. The Prophet's Salah was a reflection of his deep connection with Allah, and by following his example, believers can strive to attain that same level of devotion.

However, achieving Khushu in Salah requires consistent effort and practice. It is not enough to simply perform the physical actions of prayer without understanding their significance. To truly benefit from Salah, the worshipper must be mindful of their intentions and focus on the meanings behind the words and actions. This mindfulness is what transforms Salah from a series of motions into a powerful spiritual experience.

One of the practical ways to cultivate Khushu in Salah is to take time before the prayer to mentally prepare. Clearing the mind of distractions and focusing on the fact that one is about to stand before Allah helps to create the proper mindset for Khushu. Additionally, slowing down the movements of the prayer, allowing each posture to be fully realized, gives the heart time to reflect on the significance of each action.

In moments of distraction, the believer should gently bring their focus back to the prayer, reminding themselves of the importance of the act of worship they are engaged in. It is natural for the mind to wander, but with practice, the worshipper can train their heart to remain focused on Allah throughout the prayer. This constant effort to maintain focus is part of the journey toward achieving Khushu.

As the believer continues to develop Khushu, they will find that the effects of Salah begin to permeate other areas of their life. Salah is not an isolated act of worship; it is meant to be a source of strength and guidance for the believer's daily life. The discipline and focus cultivated in Salah help the believer to navigate the challenges of life with patience and perseverance.

Furthermore, Salah teaches humility, a quality that is essential for success in both this life and the hereafter. By bowing and prostrating before Allah, the believer is reminded of their true position in the grand scheme of existence.

This humility carries over into interactions with others, fostering kindness, generosity, and a willingness to serve. In this way, Salah acts as a constant reminder of the believer's responsibilities, both to Allah and to the creation.

In summary, the physical postures of Salah play a crucial role in fostering Khushu and deepening the believer's connection to Allah. When performed with sincerity and mindfulness, these postures become more than just actions; they become a reflection of the heart's submission to Allah's will. Through Salah, the believer is reminded of their ultimate purpose in life—to worship Allah and to live in accordance with His guidance.

The physical act of prayer serves not just as a form of worship, but as a profound reminder of the believer's relationship with their Creator. In each movement, the body reflects the state of the heart, and through this synchronization, the worshipper becomes more aware of their dependency on Allah. The act of standing, for instance, represents the believer's readiness to stand before Allah, to be judged and held accountable. It is a reminder that life itself is fleeting, and the true end lies with Allah.

This consciousness brings a deep sense of humility. When the believer places their hands on their chest, just before they bow in Ruku, it symbolizes the restraint of the self and the containment of one's worldly concerns. As the body physically turns inward, so should the heart. This moment is not one of pride but of submission, acknowledging the majesty of Allah and the insignificance of the self before His grandeur. This is the internal dialogue that must accompany the external act, making Salah a deeply transformative experience.

When Ruku is performed, the believer bends their body at the waist, with the back straightened, symbolizing a bow before Allah. This act alone speaks volumes of humility. It is a gesture that removes any sense of arrogance or self-importance, for how can one be prideful when bowing to the One who created the heavens and the earth? During this bow, the heart submits, echoing the words of the Prophet Muhammad (PBUH), who taught us to repeat, *"Subhana Rabbiyal 'Azeem"* (Glory is to my Lord, the Most Great).

When the believer rises from Ruku and stands erect once again, they are reminded of Allah's mercy. After bowing in humility, the worshipper stands straight, signifying Allah's acceptance of their submission and His mercy in allowing them to return to their original posture. The moment of stillness between Ruku and Sujood is significant, as it offers a brief respite where the believer can reflect on Allah's generosity. By saying, *"Rabbana lakal hamd"* (Our Lord, to You belongs all praise), the worshipper acknowledges that every breath, every movement, and every success in life belongs solely to Allah.

The physical postures continue as the worshipper moves into Sujood, the pinnacle of humility. In this position, the forehead touches the ground, symbolizing the total submission of the heart and body to Allah. In the Sujood, the worshipper is at their lowest point physically, but spiritually, they are at their highest. The Prophet (PBUH) taught that in Sujood, the servant is closest to their Lord. Thus, it is a moment of intense supplication and reflection. In this act of complete surrender, the believer repeats, *"Subhana Rabbiyal A'la"* (Glory is to my Lord, the Most High).

Sujood is a powerful reminder of the believer's dependence on Allah. By placing the forehead—the highest and most honored part of the body—on the ground, the worshipper demonstrates that all honor and dignity lie with Allah. This act of humility brings the believer closer to their Creator and fosters a deeper connection to the spiritual reality that underpins their existence.

The physical movements of Salah help the believer achieve a state of complete mindfulness and presence. Each posture has a distinct purpose and serves to deepen the worshipper's focus on Allah. But physical actions alone are not sufficient; they must be accompanied by the heart's engagement. Salah without Khushu is like a body without a soul. It may appear outwardly complete, but inwardly, it lacks the essence that makes it meaningful.

To cultivate Khushu, the believer must pay attention to their inner state during Salah. It is easy to fall into the habit of performing the physical movements of prayer without thinking deeply about their significance. However, the true value of Salah lies in the mindfulness that accompanies each action. When the heart is fully engaged, Salah becomes a source of tranquility, bringing the worshipper closer to Allah and helping them navigate the challenges of life with patience and clarity.

One way to enhance mindfulness during Salah is to reflect on the meanings of the words recited. Every phrase in the prayer carries deep theological and spiritual significance. For instance, the recitation of Surah Al-Fatiha in every Rak'ah is not merely a ritual, but a plea for guidance and mercy from Allah. By understanding the meaning of *"Iyyaka na'budu wa iyyaka nasta'een"* (You alone we worship, and You alone we ask for help), the worshipper is reminded of their dependence on Allah in every aspect of life.

The journey of Salah does not end with the physical movements. In fact, these movements serve as a vehicle to transport the worshipper into a state of spiritual awareness. Salah, when performed correctly, nurtures the heart and purifies the soul. Through the various postures, the believer experiences the sweetness of faith and becomes more attuned to their purpose in life.

Rising from Sujood, the believer sits briefly before returning to the second prostration. This sitting posture, known as Jalsa, is not a mere break between movements; it is a moment of reflection and calm. In Jalsa, the believer collects themselves, mentally and spiritually preparing for the next act of worship. This pause allows the heart to refocus, ensuring that the worshipper remains present in their prayer.

The second Sujood mirrors the first, once again reminding the believer of their complete reliance on Allah. By repeating the act of placing the forehead on the ground, the worshipper reinforces the message of humility and submission. This repetition serves to deepen the impact of Sujood, embedding its meaning in the heart of the believer.

The importance of slowing down the actions of Salah cannot be overstated. Often, in the rush of daily life, believers may find themselves hurrying through their prayers, eager to complete the obligation without fully experiencing its spiritual benefits. However, this rush diminishes the transformative power of Salah. By taking time with each movement and focusing on the heart's engagement, the worshipper allows Salah to fulfill its intended role as a means of purification and connection with Allah.

In moments of distraction, the believer can remind themselves of the Hadith where the Prophet (PBUH) described the Salah of the hypocrites—those who perform their prayers in haste, without Khushu. This description serves as a warning to ensure that Salah is not reduced to a set of empty actions but is performed with sincerity and mindfulness.

The final sitting posture of Tashahhud serves as a culmination of the physical and spiritual journey undertaken during Salah. Here, the believer sits before Allah, acknowledging the core tenets of faith and reaffirming their belief in the oneness of Allah and the Prophethood of Muhammad (PBUH). This moment is a powerful reminder of the worshipper's identity as a servant of Allah, dedicated to living a life in accordance with His guidance.

The Tashahhud, while short in its recitation, carries immense weight in its meaning. When the believer declares, *"Ashhadu alla ilaha illallah"* (I bear witness that there is no god but Allah), they are reaffirming the foundation of their faith. This declaration is not merely a statement of belief; it is a commitment to live a life in accordance with Tawheed. Every aspect of the believer's life should reflect this oneness, from their interactions with others to their personal conduct and inner thoughts.

Following the affirmation of Tawheed, the worshipper sends peace and blessings upon the Prophet Muhammad (PBUH). This act of sending *Salawat* is a reminder of the Prophet's role as a guide and teacher, whose example the believer strives to follow. The Prophet's life serves as the blueprint for achieving success in both this world and the hereafter. By sending peace upon him, the believer expresses gratitude for the guidance he brought and seeks Allah's mercy in living up to the standard he set.

After the declaration of Tawheed and sending blessings upon the Prophet Muhammad (PBUH), the worshipper enters the final moments of Salah. These last moments are just as important as the first. The conclusion of the prayer is marked by the turning of the head to the right and then to the left while saying *"Assalamu Alaikum wa Rahmatullah"* (Peace and mercy of Allah be upon you). This act is not only a means of concluding the prayer, but it also signifies the believer's connection to the rest of the Muslim community. By sending peace to those around them, the worshipper acknowledges their role within the Ummah and their responsibility towards their fellow believers.

This closing of the prayer is a moment of calm reflection. After the intense spiritual journey that Salah represents, the worshipper now steps back into the world, carrying with them the tranquility and focus that prayer has instilled. It serves as a reminder that although the physical act of Salah has ended, the lessons and the spiritual state attained during it should carry over into daily life. The believer's connection with Allah does not end with Salah; rather, it is strengthened and carried forward into every action and decision.

Moreover, the act of sending peace at the end of Salah also reminds the believer that Islam is a religion of peace. It is a way of life that fosters harmony not only between the worshipper and their Creator but also between individuals in the community. The believer is encouraged to be a source of peace, spreading tranquility and kindness in their interactions with others, reflecting the essence of Salah in their behavior.

The significance of Salah in shaping the believer's character is profound. Each of the physical postures, from standing in Qiyam to the final Tasleem, is a reminder of the believer's submission, humility, and commitment to living a life aligned with the principles of Islam. Salah is not merely a ritual; it is a transformative experience that refines the soul and nurtures the heart. Through regular and sincere prayer, the believer becomes more mindful of their purpose in life and more conscious of their relationship with Allah.

Salah serves as a training ground for the believer. The discipline it instills—both in terms of physical postures and mental focus—extends beyond the boundaries of prayer. A believer who cultivates Khushu in their Salah is more likely to practice patience, mindfulness, and humility in their daily life. They become more aware of their actions, more reflective about their choices, and more deliberate in their interactions with others. The spiritual benefits of Salah, therefore, transcend the prayer itself and shape the believer's overall character and approach to life.

In addition to the personal benefits of Salah, it also strengthens the bonds of the Muslim community. The collective performance of Salah, especially in congregation, fosters a sense of unity and brotherhood among believers. When Muslims stand shoulder to shoulder in prayer, their differences in wealth, status, or nationality become irrelevant. They are united in their worship of Allah, bound together by their shared faith. This unity is a reflection of the broader Islamic principle of community and mutual support, encouraging believers to look out for one another and work together for the common good.

The effect of Salah on the believer's soul cannot be overstated. Each time the worshipper enters into Salah with sincerity and focus, they are drawing closer to Allah. The physical postures serve as a constant reminder of this closeness, reinforcing the connection between the worshipper and their Creator. Salah, when performed with Khushu, becomes a source of immense peace and solace. It is a sanctuary from the chaos of the world, a moment where the believer can turn inward and reflect on their relationship with Allah.

This inward reflection is crucial for spiritual growth. Salah provides the believer with a regular opportunity to assess their own state of faith and to seek Allah's guidance in improving their character and conduct. Through prayer, the believer is reminded of their dependence on Allah, and this reminder fosters a sense of humility and gratitude. It encourages the believer to rely on Allah in times of difficulty and to be grateful for His blessings in times of ease.

Furthermore, Salah is a source of strength for the believer. Life is full of challenges, and it is easy to become overwhelmed by the difficulties that arise. However, Salah provides the believer with a regular means of seeking Allah's help and mercy. It is a moment of refuge, where the worshipper can pour out their heart to Allah and find comfort in knowing that He is always there, listening and ready to assist.

The ultimate goal of Salah is to bring the believer closer to Allah. The physical postures, the recitation of Quranic verses, and the supplications made during prayer are all designed to foster a deep sense of connection and reliance on Allah. This connection is not limited to the moments of Salah but should extend into every aspect of the believer's life. A believer who performs Salah with Khushu is more likely to live a life that is aligned with the teachings of Islam, a life that is rooted in Tawheed and dedicated to seeking Allah's pleasure.

As the believer continues to cultivate Khushu in their Salah, they will begin to notice its effects in other areas of their life. They will become more patient, more mindful, and more aware of their responsibilities as a servant of Allah. This heightened awareness will help them to navigate life's challenges with greater clarity and resilience, knowing that Allah is always with them, guiding them and supporting them.

In conclusion, Salah is more than just a physical act of worship; it is a powerful means of spiritual purification and growth. Through the physical postures of Salah, the believer is reminded of their humility before Allah, their dependence on His mercy, and their commitment to living a life of righteousness. By performing Salah with sincerity and Khushu, the believer not only strengthens their relationship with Allah but also refines their character, becoming a source of peace and guidance for others. May Allah grant us all the ability to perform our Salah with Khushu and accept our efforts in His worship.

8: **THE DANGERS OF HASTINESS IN SALAH**

The act of Salah, central to the life of every Muslim, is one that demands reverence, calm, and focus. However, one of the most frequent and damaging mistakes that many believers fall into is hastiness during prayer. When a person rushes through Salah, they are denying themselves the opportunity to truly connect with Allah and reflect on the words and movements that form the core of the prayer. This hastiness strips Salah of its intended purpose, transforming it into a hurried ritual rather than a moment of deep spiritual reflection and submission.

Hastiness in Salah is often driven by external distractions—be it the pull of worldly responsibilities, time constraints, or the mind wandering to other matters. Yet, this hurried approach diminishes the value of the prayer and can even lead to errors in performing essential acts like Ruku (bowing) and Sujood (prostration). The Prophet Muhammad (PBUH) warned about this, reminding believers that Salah is not simply about completing the motions but about achieving a state of mindfulness and humility before Allah.

In rushing through prayer, believers not only fail to fulfill the external aspects of Salah correctly, such as the proper posture and length of time in each position, but they also lose the internal essence of Khushu (focus and humility). When Khushu is absent, the prayer becomes empty, devoid of the spiritual nourishment that it is meant to provide.

The Prophet Muhammad (PBUH) was known for his deep concentration and tranquility during Salah. He would perform each movement with measured calmness, ensuring that every part of the prayer was completed properly and with full attention. The Messenger of Allah once saw a man rushing through his Salah, hastily performing the Ruku and Sujood without giving them their due time. The Prophet (PBUH) advised him, "Go back and pray, for you have not prayed." This hadith underscores the critical importance of taking one's time during Salah.

The essence of prayer lies in its ability to connect the believer to Allah. The calmness that one brings to their prayer is a reflection of their understanding of this sacred connection. Hastiness, on the other hand, reflects a lack of understanding of the immense value of the time spent in Salah. Allah has granted these moments as opportunities to draw closer to Him, and they should not be wasted in rushed and distracted motions.

Furthermore, when a person prays hastily, they miss out on the benefits that each part of the prayer offers. The act of standing in Qiyam, bowing in Ruku, and prostrating in Sujood all hold profound spiritual significance. Each position is a reminder of the believer's humility, submission, and dependence on Allah. Rushing through these actions diminishes their meaning and impact on the heart.

One of the key reasons believers fall into the trap of hastiness in Salah is the pervasive influence of modern life, where time is constantly in short supply, and distractions are endless. The world encourages speed, efficiency, and multitasking—concepts that are contrary to the essence of Salah. Prayer is meant to slow down time, to offer a reprieve from the busyness of life, and to remind the believer of their ultimate purpose: worshiping Allah.

To combat the tendency toward hastiness, it is essential for believers to prepare themselves mentally and spiritually before entering into prayer. A few moments of reflection, remembrance of Allah, or recitation of Quranic verses can help clear the mind and focus the heart. The Prophet (PBUH) would always approach prayer with a sense of calm and preparation, ensuring that his heart and mind were fully engaged in worship.

Additionally, believers should be mindful of the amount of time they allocate for Salah. By giving themselves sufficient time, they reduce the likelihood of rushing through the prayer. Instead of seeing Salah as an interruption to their daily activities, it should be viewed as the central event around which the day is structured. This mindset shift allows for greater focus and reverence during the prayer, making it a priority rather than a task to be hurried through.

The consequences of hastiness in Salah go beyond the prayer itself. When a person consistently rushes through their prayers, they may find that their connection to Allah weakens over time. The spiritual nourishment that Salah provides is gradually lost, and the believer may begin to feel a sense of emptiness or detachment in their relationship with their Creator. Salah is meant to be a source of strength, guidance, and comfort, but this can only be achieved when it is performed with sincerity, focus, and calmness.

Moreover, the habit of hastiness can extend to other areas of a believer's life. Just as they rush through their Salah, they may begin to rush through their daily interactions, neglecting important moments of reflection and connection with others. Hastiness in prayer can lead to hastiness in thought, speech, and action, affecting the overall quality of a person's life.

Islam teaches the importance of patience, calmness, and reflection in all matters, and this is particularly true in Salah. The believer is encouraged to approach every action with deliberation, ensuring that their intentions are sincere and their efforts are meaningful. Salah is a training ground for this mindset, offering believers the opportunity to cultivate patience, mindfulness, and humility in their daily lives.

Another critical issue with hastiness in Salah is the risk of invalidating the prayer. When a person rushes through the movements of Salah without giving each posture its due time, they may inadvertently fail to meet the minimum requirements of the prayer. For example, the Ruku and Sujood must be performed with a certain level of calmness and stillness, allowing the body to fully settle into each position. Rushing through these postures can result in an incomplete or invalid prayer.

This is why the Prophet Muhammad (PBUH) emphasized the importance of taking one's time in Salah. He would often instruct his companions to lengthen their prayers, to ensure that every movement was performed correctly, and to engage their hearts fully in the worship of Allah. A prayer that is rushed is one that may not be accepted by Allah, as it lacks the sincerity and focus that are required for true worship.

In addition to invalidating the prayer, hastiness can also lead to a lack of understanding of the meanings behind the words and actions of Salah. The Quranic verses recited during prayer are meant to be reflected upon, and the supplications made in Sujood and Tashahhud are moments for deep personal connection with Allah. When a person rushes through these parts of the prayer, they miss the opportunity to truly engage with the meanings and significance of the words they are saying.

The essence of Salah is to cultivate a deep connection with Allah through moments of tranquility and reflection. Hastiness erodes this connection, reducing the prayer to a series of rushed physical movements rather than a meaningful spiritual act. Each aspect of Salah, from the Takbir to the Salam, has its own significance, and performing these actions with haste deprives the believer of the full experience of submitting to their Creator.

Hastiness in Salah is particularly problematic because it can become a habit. When a person repeatedly rushes through their prayers, they become accustomed to this hurried pace, and it becomes increasingly difficult to slow down and engage in a more thoughtful and deliberate manner. Breaking this cycle requires conscious effort and a shift in mindset. The believer must remind themselves of the value of prayer and the immense blessings that come with performing it properly and with devotion.

To cultivate a deeper sense of calm and mindfulness in Salah, it is important for believers to approach each prayer as if it could be their last. This was the practice of the Prophet Muhammad (PBUH), who encouraged his followers to pray as though they were bidding farewell to the world. When a person prays with this mindset, they are more likely to take their time, focus on the words and movements, and engage their hearts fully in worship.

One practical way to avoid hastiness in Salah is to set aside specific times for prayer, free from distractions. In today's world, where people are constantly connected to their phones, work, and social media, it can be difficult to find moments of uninterrupted peace. However, Salah is a time for disconnecting from the world and reconnecting with Allah. By creating an environment that is conducive to focus and reflection, believers can reduce the temptation to rush through their prayers.

Additionally, it is helpful to remember that Salah is not merely an obligation but a privilege. Allah, in His mercy, has given believers the opportunity to come before Him in prayer five times a day. Each of these moments is a chance to seek forgiveness, guidance, and comfort from the Creator. When a person views Salah through this lens, they are less likely to rush through it and more likely to cherish the time spent in prayer.

Another beneficial practice is to recite the Quran with concentration and understanding during Salah. When the heart and mind are engaged in the meanings of the Quranic verses, it becomes easier to slow down and appreciate the words being recited. The Prophet (PBUH) often reminded his companions of the importance of reciting the Quran with reflection and humility, rather than simply rushing through the verses.

The Prophet Muhammad (PBUH) also emphasized the importance of performing each movement in Salah with precision. From standing in Qiyam to the prostration of Sujood, every movement in prayer carries meaning and significance. The Ruku, for instance, is a moment of deep humility before Allah, where the believer bows down, acknowledging their dependence on their Creator. In Sujood, the believer places their forehead on the ground, symbolizing total submission to Allah's will. By rushing through these movements, a person fails to express the humility and submission that are central to Salah.

Moreover, the moments between movements—such as the pause between Ruku and Sujood—are equally important. These moments allow the believer to reflect on their worship and ensure that their body and mind are fully settled before moving on to the next part of the prayer. Hastiness often results in skipping these pauses, leading to a rushed and incomplete prayer.

To remedy this, believers should focus on maintaining stillness and calmness in every movement of Salah. This includes not only the physical stillness of the body but also the stillness of the heart and mind. The Prophet (PBUH) described Khushu as an essential element of Salah, where the heart is fully engaged in the act of worship, and the believer is mindful of their words and actions.

Another important aspect of avoiding hastiness in Salah is being mindful of the time allocated for prayer. Allah, in His wisdom, has prescribed specific times for each of the five daily prayers, allowing sufficient time for believers to perform them without rushing. By planning their day around the prayer times, believers can ensure that they have enough time to perform their Salah properly and without distraction.

When a person waits until the last possible moment to pray, they are more likely to rush through it in an attempt to complete it before the time expires. This is a common mistake that can be avoided by performing prayers earlier in their designated time window. The Prophet (PBUH) often encouraged believers to pray at the beginning of the prayer time, as this not only allows for more focus but also demonstrates a prioritization of worship over worldly concerns.

In addition to performing Salah on time, it is also beneficial to lengthen the prayer. While it is not required to spend an extended amount of time in each prayer, taking a few extra moments in Ruku, Sujood, and Tashahhud can significantly enhance the quality of the prayer. This additional time allows for deeper reflection on the words being recited and strengthens the connection between the believer and Allah.

The importance of maintaining calmness and focus in Salah cannot be overstated. Salah is not only a physical act but also an emotional and spiritual experience. It is through this experience that believers draw closer to Allah, seek His guidance, and express their gratitude for His countless blessings. Rushing through Salah, on the other hand, robs the believer of this profound opportunity for spiritual growth.

One of the primary goals of Salah is to achieve a sense of peace and tranquility, both during the prayer and after it. When a person prays with mindfulness and humility, they are more likely to carry the effects of that prayer into the rest of their day. This sense of peace can help believers navigate the challenges of life with greater patience, wisdom, and reliance on Allah.

Conversely, when Salah is rushed, it is less likely to have a lasting impact on the believer's heart and actions. The peace and tranquility that come from a well-performed prayer are often absent in a hurried prayer, leaving the believer feeling disconnected from the spiritual benefits of Salah.

Salah is meant to be an intimate conversation between the servant and Allah. When performed with care and deliberation, it becomes a time for reflection, repentance, and renewal of faith. In this sacred space, the believer can find solace in knowing that they are standing before their Creator, seeking His mercy and guidance. Rushing through this moment of connection is a disservice not only to the worshipper but also to the essence of Salah itself.

The Prophet (PBUH) demonstrated the importance of taking time in prayer by his own actions. In many narrations, it is mentioned that his Salah was neither too long nor too short, but always measured and balanced. He would ensure that each part of the prayer was given its due respect, whether it was reciting Surah Al-Fatiha or performing Sujood. This was done not only for his own spiritual benefit but also to set an example for his followers on how to perform Salah with dignity and focus.

In following the Sunnah, believers can avoid the pitfalls of hastiness and ensure that their prayers are meaningful. By imitating the Prophet's method of prayer, they are engaging in an act of worship that is rooted in humility and consciousness of Allah's greatness. Every Ruku and every Sujood becomes a reminder of the servant's position before their Lord, a position that requires patience, sincerity, and focus.

The beauty of Salah lies in its ability to transform the heart. However, this transformation can only occur when the heart is fully present in the prayer. When the mind is preoccupied with worldly concerns or when the body rushes through the movements, the transformative power of Salah is diminished. On the contrary, when the believer approaches Salah with calmness and sincerity, their heart is softened, and their faith is strengthened.

The Prophet (PBUH) often reminded his companions of the importance of Khushu'—the state of humility and concentration in Salah. Khushu' is not just about physical stillness but also about the state of the heart and mind. When a person has Khushu', their focus is entirely on Allah, and they are able to perform each movement of the prayer with the awareness that they are standing before their Creator.

This state of mindfulness is difficult to achieve when a person rushes through their prayers. Instead of focusing on the words being recited or the significance of each movement, the mind is distracted, and the body is simply going through the motions. To cultivate Khushu', the believer must make a conscious effort to slow down, reflect on the words of the Quran, and remind themselves of the immense privilege it is to stand before Allah in prayer.

It is essential to recognize that Salah is not just a ritualistic obligation, but a means of connecting with Allah. Each prayer is an opportunity for the believer to realign their focus, seek forgiveness, and draw closer to their Creator. When this opportunity is approached with haste, it becomes less about the spiritual connection and more about fulfilling a duty.

The Prophet (PBUH) warned against this kind of mechanical approach to prayer. In several Hadiths, he emphasized the importance of taking one's time in Salah and ensuring that every movement is performed with care. One such narration mentions a man who prayed hastily, and the Prophet (PBUH) instructed him to pray again, explaining that the speed with which he performed the prayer rendered it invalid. This underscores the importance of performing Salah with proper attention to both its outward form and inner significance.

One of the reasons people may feel rushed in their prayers is the pressure of time. With busy schedules and countless distractions, it can be challenging to find moments of calm to dedicate to Salah. However, this challenge is precisely why the five daily prayers are spread throughout the day. They offer believers a chance to pause, reflect, and reconnect with Allah in the midst of their daily responsibilities. By making Salah a priority and carving out time for it, believers can ensure that they are able to perform it without haste.

The Prophet (PBUH) also taught that prayer is an opportunity for forgiveness. Each time a person stands before Allah in Salah, they are given a chance to seek pardon for their sins and shortcomings. However, this act of seeking forgiveness requires sincerity and focus. When a person rushes through their prayers, they may miss the opportunity to truly reflect on their mistakes and seek Allah's mercy.

One of the most powerful aspects of Salah is that it serves as a daily reminder of the believer's dependence on Allah. Each time a person bows in Ruku or prostrates in Sujood, they are acknowledging their need for Allah's guidance and forgiveness. This sense of humility is difficult to cultivate when prayers are performed hastily. The very act of slowing down and taking time in Salah reinforces the believer's recognition of their need for Allah's mercy and grace.

Furthermore, Salah is a form of protection against the evils of the world. Allah says in the Quran: "Indeed, prayer prohibits immorality and wrongdoing" (Surah Al-Ankabut, 29:45). However, for Salah to fulfill this role, it must be performed with mindfulness and sincerity. A rushed and distracted prayer is less likely to have this transformative effect on the heart and mind. By taking time in Salah, believers allow its spiritual benefits to take root in their lives, guiding them towards righteousness and away from sin.

In the pursuit of a more meaningful and impactful prayer, it is important to focus not only on the physical aspects of Salah but also on its emotional and spiritual dimensions. Salah is an act of submission, and each movement symbolizes a different aspect of this submission. For instance, when a person stands in Qiyam, they are standing before their Creator in obedience. When they bow in Ruku, they are demonstrating their humility before Allah. When they prostrate in Sujood, they are expressing their total submission to Allah's will.

By reflecting on the meanings behind each movement, believers can enhance their focus and avoid the trap of hastiness. Instead of rushing through the motions, they can take their time to engage with each part of the prayer, deepening their connection with Allah in the process.

One practical way to slow down in Salah is to extend the time spent in Sujood. The Prophet (PBUH) described Sujood as the moment when a person is closest to Allah. It is during Sujood that believers can make sincere du'a, asking for Allah's forgiveness, guidance, and blessings. By spending more time in Sujood, believers can strengthen their relationship with Allah and experience the tranquility that comes from heartfelt submission.

Sujood is one of the most profound parts of Salah. It is an act of complete submission and humility, where the worshipper places the most honored part of their body, the face, on the ground before their Creator. The Prophet (PBUH) emphasized the importance of this position, stating that a servant is closest to Allah when they are in Sujood. This closeness is not only physical but also spiritual. In this moment, a believer's heart is open, and they can pour out their thoughts, fears, hopes, and requests to their Lord.

Rushing through Sujood or treating it as a mere requirement to check off diminishes the essence of this powerful moment. The one who understands the significance of Sujood will approach it with eagerness and sincerity, knowing that it is an opportunity to seek Allah's mercy and blessings. It is in these moments of complete humility that Allah answers the prayers of His servants, granting them relief from their hardships and strength to overcome the trials of life.

Believers must remind themselves that each Sujood is an opportunity to seek forgiveness, to reflect on their shortcomings, and to ask for guidance. By prolonging Sujood and making heartfelt du'a, the worshipper not only fulfills the outward obligations of prayer but also deepens their relationship with Allah.

The importance of not rushing through Salah is further highlighted by the Prophet's (PBUH) instruction to his companions. He would remind them that Salah is the believer's connection with Allah, and that it should be treated as a priority, not as a burdensome obligation. In one narration, the Prophet (PBUH) said, "The first matter that the slave will be brought to account for on the Day of Judgment is the prayer. If it is sound, then the rest of his deeds will be sound; and if it is corrupt, then the rest of his deeds will be corrupt."

This narration should serve as a powerful reminder of the importance of Salah in the life of a believer. It is the foundation of their relationship with Allah and the measure by which other deeds are judged. Thus, rushing through this fundamental act of worship diminishes its value and risks rendering it ineffective.

To ensure that one's Salah is accepted and valued, it is essential to approach it with sincerity, focus, and dedication. Haste in Salah reflects a lack of appreciation for its significance and a failure to recognize the opportunity it offers for spiritual growth and closeness to Allah.

Another key point to remember is the communal aspect of Salah. While much of the focus is on personal prayer and the connection between the individual and Allah, there is also a communal dimension, especially in the congregational prayers. When praying in congregation, believers are encouraged to follow the imam closely but with attentiveness. The imam leads the prayer at a moderate pace, ensuring that each movement is performed correctly and that the congregation can follow with ease.

However, some may feel inclined to rush ahead of the imam, performing the Ruku or Sujood before the imam completes his movement. This is a form of hastiness that not only disrupts the flow of the congregational prayer but also shows a lack of discipline. The Prophet (PBUH) emphasized that the one following the imam should not precede him in any movement. Instead, they should wait for the imam to initiate the next position before following. This practice not only fosters unity within the congregation but also instills patience and mindfulness in each participant.

In individual prayers, the same principle applies. Each movement of Salah should be deliberate and measured. By resisting the urge to rush, the believer can fully engage with the prayer and experience its spiritual benefits.

Salah is not merely a physical exercise or a set of rituals to be performed mindlessly. It is a powerful tool for self-reflection and self-improvement. Each prayer is an opportunity to recalibrate one's focus, to leave behind the distractions of the world, and to reconnect with Allah. Rushing through Salah robs the believer of this opportunity and limits the positive impact it can have on their life.

One of the reasons people may find themselves rushing through Salah is because they feel overwhelmed by worldly responsibilities. Work, family, and personal obligations may seem all-consuming, leaving little time for quiet reflection or worship. However, it is precisely because of these responsibilities that Salah is so crucial. It offers a moment of respite from the busyness of life and allows the believer to realign their priorities.

By slowing down in Salah, the worshipper is making a conscious decision to prioritize their relationship with Allah over the temporary concerns of this world. They are acknowledging that no matter how pressing their worldly affairs may be, their connection with Allah is more important. This shift in focus brings peace and clarity, allowing the believer to navigate their responsibilities with greater ease and confidence.

In conclusion, the believer must recognize the dangers of hastiness in Salah and strive to overcome them. Prayer is the cornerstone of faith, the daily reminder of our purpose, and the direct connection between the servant and their Creator. To treat it with anything less than complete sincerity and focus is to diminish its value and miss out on its transformative power.

By slowing down, paying attention to each movement, and engaging with the words being recited, the believer can unlock the true potential of Salah. It becomes not just a ritual, but a means of spiritual growth, self-improvement, and closeness to Allah. The one who approaches Salah with mindfulness and care will find peace in their heart, clarity in their mind, and strength in their soul.

Let every prayer be an opportunity to seek Allah's mercy, to reflect on His greatness, and to renew one's commitment to living a life of righteousness and devotion.

9: THE ROLE OF STILLNESS AND CALMNESS IN SALAH

In Salah, every action, movement, and word has profound meaning and purpose. Yet, it is in stillness and calmness that one finds the deeper connection with Allah. The tranquility of Salah is a reflection of the heart's submission, an external manifestation of inner peace. The more calm and composed a person is in their prayer, the more focused their heart becomes, and the easier it is to attain Khushu, the sense of awe and humility that makes Salah spiritually powerful.

The Prophet Muhammad (PBUH) consistently emphasized the importance of performing each movement of Salah with deliberation and calm. The perfection of Salah is not in its speed or efficiency but in how each Ruku, Sujood, and every stance is performed with the fullness of attention. One hadith mentions, "The worst thief is the one who steals from his prayer." When asked how this is possible, the Prophet (PBUH) responded, "He does not complete his Ruku and Sujood properly."

The significance of stillness in Salah lies in its ability to help the worshipper focus on their connection with Allah. When the body moves calmly, without haste or rush, the mind and heart can synchronize with that pace, allowing deeper reflection on the words being recited and the purpose of the prayer itself. It is in this calm that one can truly experience the essence of Salah.

Stillness, however, does not only pertain to the outward physical movements. It also refers to the stillness of the heart. A heart that is filled with the distractions of the world cannot attain true Khushu. The believer must strive to still their heart from the noise of worldly concerns when standing before Allah. This inward calm is the key to unlocking a higher level of focus and sincerity in Salah.

In the Qur'an, Allah speaks about the qualities of the believers who attain success. Among these qualities, He mentions, "They are those who are humble in their prayers" (Surah Al-Mu'minun, 23:2). The term 'humble' here refers to a state of being fully present, both outwardly and inwardly, in prayer. Such humility comes from stillness—being present in the moment, free from distractions, and fully aware of standing before the Creator.

This concept of stillness can also be seen in the Sunnah of the Prophet (PBUH). He would often pause between movements in Salah, allowing a moment of reflection before moving on to the next part of the prayer. For example, after rising from Ruku, he would stand still and straight, taking the time to glorify Allah before proceeding to Sujood. This moment of calm is critical because it reflects the true purpose of prayer: to connect with Allah with full concentration and reverence.

The way one approaches Salah is a reflection of their understanding of its significance. A person who rushes through their prayers, without giving time for stillness and reflection, demonstrates a lack of awareness of the gravity of standing before Allah. The Prophet (PBUH) warned against such hastiness, as it diminishes the spiritual benefits of Salah and can lead to negligence in fulfilling its requirements.

It is narrated in a hadith that the Prophet (PBUH) once saw a man performing Salah hastily, without allowing time for stillness between movements. The Prophet (PBUH) told him to repeat his prayer, saying, "Go back and pray, for you have not prayed." The man repeated his prayer several times, but each time the Prophet (PBUH) gave him the same instruction. Finally, the Prophet (PBUH) explained to him the correct way to perform Salah, emphasizing the importance of stillness and calmness in every movement.

The lesson here is clear: stillness is not optional in Salah; it is a fundamental part of the prayer. Without it, the prayer loses its essence, and the worshipper fails to experience the spiritual depth that comes from a properly performed Salah. It is through calmness and deliberate action that a person can fully engage in their prayer, allowing their heart to connect with their Creator.

In addition to the spiritual benefits of stillness, there are practical advantages as well. When one performs Salah with calmness, it helps to avoid mistakes and ensures that each movement is done correctly. This is particularly important in the case of Ruku and Sujood, where physical actions are closely tied to the validity of the prayer. For example, if a person rushes through Ruku without properly bowing or standing up straight afterward, their Salah may be invalid.

Furthermore, performing Salah with stillness allows for greater reflection on the meaning of the words being recited. When one takes their time in

Salah, they are more likely to ponder the words of the Qur'an, to reflect on Allah's greatness, and to make sincere du'a. This reflection is essential for developing Khushu and for transforming Salah into a meaningful act of worship rather than a mere routine.

Stillness also brings with it a sense of peace and relaxation. The modern world is filled with stress and distractions, and many people struggle to find moments of calm in their day-to-day lives. Salah, when performed with the right mindset, provides an opportunity to step away from the busyness of life and to find inner peace. The deliberate, slow movements of Salah, combined with the focus on Allah, help to calm the mind and soothe the heart.

One of the challenges many people face when trying to maintain stillness in Salah is the temptation to rush. This is often due to external factors such as time constraints or the presence of distractions in the environment. However, it is essential to remember that Salah is not merely a task to be completed; it is an opportunity to connect with Allah and to find peace in His remembrance.

To cultivate stillness in Salah, one must consciously work on removing distractions and creating an environment conducive to focus. This may involve finding a quiet place to pray, setting aside enough time to complete Salah without feeling rushed, and mentally preparing oneself for the act of worship. By taking these steps, a person can create the right conditions for stillness and calmness in their prayer.

Moreover, it is helpful to remind oneself of the reward that comes with performing Salah with focus and calmness. The Prophet (PBUH) said, "The closest that a servant comes to his Lord is when he is prostrating." In Sujood, the heart is open, and the servant is in a state of complete humility before Allah. This is a moment to be savored, not rushed. By remaining still in Sujood and reflecting on the greatness of Allah, one can deepen their connection with Him and attain a higher level of Khushu.

Another essential aspect of stillness in Salah is the effect it has on the worshipper's state of mind. When the body is calm, the mind follows. A calm mind is more likely to focus on the words being recited, to contemplate their meaning, and to engage in sincere reflection. Conversely, a restless body leads to a restless mind, and the worshipper becomes easily distracted by thoughts of the dunya.

This connection between physical stillness and mental focus is one of the reasons why the Prophet (PBUH) emphasized performing each movement of Salah with precision and care. By taking the time to perform each Ruku and Sujood properly, the worshipper is also training their mind to focus on the prayer and to avoid distractions. This practice of mindfulness in Salah can have a transformative effect on a person's overall spiritual life, helping them to develop a greater sense of awareness of Allah in all aspects of their life.

Finally, it is essential to recognize that stillness in Salah is not about being perfect. Every person will have moments of distraction or lapses in focus. What is important is the effort to improve and to approach Salah with sincerity and dedication. By making a conscious effort to slow down, to focus, and to remain still, a person can gradually develop a more profound connection with Allah through their prayer.

When discussing stillness in Salah, it is essential to reflect on the profound spiritual transformation that occurs when one takes the time to offer prayers with the right attitude. The act of being still before Allah is a recognition of His immense power and control over all things. It is an acknowledgment of the believer's dependence on the Creator, as well as a submission to His will. This mindset transforms Salah from a mere routine into an act of devotion that deeply impacts both the body and soul.

Moreover, stillness in Salah is not limited to the physical body. It also extends to the inner being, particularly the thoughts and emotions of the worshipper. The distractions of life often cloud our hearts and minds during prayer. Whether it is the stress of work, family matters, or other concerns, these thoughts can easily pull the heart away from Allah. This is why cultivating inner stillness—focusing entirely on Allah and the words being recited—is critical to experiencing the true beauty of Salah.

The Prophet Muhammad (PBUH) described Salah as the "coolness of the eyes." This expression highlights the peace and tranquility that prayer should bring to a person's heart and mind. When the body is still, and the heart is focused, the believer experiences a sense of contentment and relief. Salah becomes a retreat from the worries of the world, a time to reconnect with the Creator and find solace in His remembrance.

Attaining stillness in Salah requires both practice and patience. It is a skill that must be developed over time. One way to cultivate stillness is by taking a moment before beginning Salah to mentally prepare oneself for the act of worship. This could involve reflecting on the greatness of Allah, seeking forgiveness for any shortcomings, and reminding oneself of the ultimate purpose of life—to worship Allah. By taking this brief moment of preparation, the worshipper can enter Salah with a clearer mind and a greater sense of purpose.

Additionally, focusing on the words being recited during Salah can help bring about inner calmness. Understanding the meanings of the verses from the Qur'an, the supplications in Ruku and Sujood, and the phrases of praise and glorification deepens the worshipper's connection with the prayer. This connection, in turn, fosters stillness because the mind becomes engaged with the meaning of the words, leaving little room for distractions.

Stillness in Salah also provides an opportunity for self-reflection. As the worshipper stands before Allah in humility and awe, they should consider their own state of faith, their relationship with Allah, and the path they are walking in life. This moment of reflection allows the believer to realign themselves with their ultimate purpose and renew their commitment to living a life of devotion and obedience to Allah.

One of the greatest benefits of stillness in Salah is its impact on Khushu, the sense of awe, humility, and concentration that every believer strives for in prayer. Without stillness, it is difficult to attain Khushu. When the body is restless, and the mind is filled with distractions, the heart cannot fully engage in the prayer. On the other hand, when the body is calm and the mind is focused, Khushu naturally follows.

It is also important to recognize that achieving stillness in Salah is not something that happens overnight. It is a gradual process that requires persistence and dedication. The Prophet Muhammad (PBUH) himself emphasized the need for patience in worship, and this applies to Salah as well. One must consistently strive to improve the quality of their prayer, focusing on both the outward actions and the inner state of the heart.

A practical way to develop stillness in Salah is by incorporating moments of pause between movements. After completing each action, whether it be Ruku, Sujood, or standing, the worshipper should take a moment to reflect on the significance of that movement and to engage in remembrance of Allah. For instance, after rising from Ruku, one should stand still for a few seconds, praising Allah before moving into Sujood. This deliberate pause not only enhances focus but also reminds the worshipper of the immense importance of each movement in Salah.

Another key aspect of achieving stillness in Salah is creating an environment that minimizes distractions. The place where one prays should be free from noise, visual distractions, and other interruptions. This is especially important in today's fast-paced world, where distractions are abundant. By choosing a quiet, clean, and peaceful space for Salah, the worshipper can create the conditions necessary for stillness and focus.

Moreover, technology has become one of the biggest sources of distraction during prayer. The constant notifications from phones, tablets, or other devices can easily disrupt one's concentration in Salah. Therefore, it is crucial to put away such devices before beginning prayer, ensuring that the mind remains focused solely on worship. By taking these practical steps, a person can create a peaceful environment that supports their efforts to attain stillness in Salah.

The Prophet (PBUH) once said, "When one of you prays, he is in a private conversation with his Lord." This profound statement reminds us that Salah is not simply a series of physical movements or spoken words. It is an intimate dialogue with Allah, where the believer has the opportunity to connect deeply with their Creator. Achieving stillness in both body and heart enhances this dialogue, allowing the worshipper to experience a more meaningful and spiritually fulfilling prayer.

Stillness in Salah also has a significant impact on the spiritual and emotional well-being of the believer. When a person takes the time to perform each movement with care and deliberation, they experience a sense of peace that extends beyond the prayer itself. This peace carries over into other aspects of life, helping the believer to approach challenges and difficulties with a calm and composed mindset.

Furthermore, stillness allows for greater mindfulness and presence in the moment. In our busy lives, it is easy to become consumed by worries about the future or regrets about the past. Salah, when performed with stillness and focus, offers a refuge from these concerns. It brings the worshipper into the present moment, allowing them to disconnect from the worries of the world and reconnect with Allah.

This mindfulness in Salah can also have a positive effect on other forms of worship. When a person learns to focus and remain still in prayer, they develop the ability to be more mindful and present in other acts of worship, such as reading Qur'an, making du'a, or engaging in acts of charity. Thus, the stillness cultivated in Salah becomes a tool for personal growth and spiritual development.

The benefits of stillness in Salah extend beyond the individual worshipper. When a community prays together in stillness and tranquility, it fosters a sense of unity and spiritual connection among the worshippers. The collective act of standing together before Allah, each person striving to perfect their prayer, creates an atmosphere of reverence and humility. This shared experience strengthens the bonds of brotherhood and sisterhood within the community and reinforces the importance of Salah as a central pillar of Islamic life.

In the context of communal prayer, stillness is particularly important for the Imam. The Imam is responsible for leading the congregation in prayer, and their movements set the pace for the rest of the worshippers. If the Imam rushes through the prayer without allowing time for stillness, it affects the entire congregation. On the other hand, an Imam who takes their time and performs each movement with care sets a positive example for the congregation, encouraging them to do the same.

Therefore, both the Imam and the congregation must strive for stillness and calmness in Salah. By doing so, they can create an environment that is conducive to spiritual growth and reflection, allowing each worshipper to experience the full benefits of prayer.

The importance of stillness in Salah extends beyond the spiritual and emotional aspects; it also impacts the physical form of the prayer. When movements in Salah are rushed or performed carelessly, it diminishes the overall integrity of the prayer. Islam emphasizes the importance of balance in every aspect of life, and Salah is no exception. Each movement in the prayer—whether it is the bowing in Ruku, the prostration in Sujood, or the standing position—should be performed with precision and mindfulness.

Proper stillness in each of these movements reflects the believer's respect for the act of worship itself. The Prophet Muhammad (PBUH) emphasized this in several narrations, encouraging believers to perfect their Salah by being mindful of their physical actions. This is not merely a ritualistic requirement but rather a means of ensuring that the entire body, mind, and soul are aligned in devotion to Allah.

In Ruku, for instance, the believer should bow completely, keeping the back straight and the hands firmly placed on the knees. It is not enough to simply dip down and rise quickly. The bowing position should be maintained for a few moments, allowing the worshipper to reflect on the greatness of Allah. Likewise, in Sujood, the forehead and nose must touch the ground, and the believer should take the time to rest in this posture, feeling the profound humility that comes from prostrating before Allah.

The relationship between physical stillness and inner tranquility is evident throughout the various positions of Salah. When the body is at peace, it helps to calm the mind and heart, allowing the worshipper to engage more deeply in the prayer. This is why it is essential to give each position of the prayer its due right. The Prophet (PBUH) once advised a man who rushed through his Salah by saying, "Go back and pray, for you have not prayed." This instruction highlights the significance of performing each movement with care and focus.

The value of stillness in prayer is not only tied to the perfection of the outward actions but also to the quality of the believer's relationship with Allah. Salah is a means of communicating with Allah, and just as we would not rush through a conversation with someone important to us, we should not rush through our prayer. Each word, each movement, and each moment spent in Salah is an opportunity to draw closer to Allah and to seek His mercy and guidance.

This connection between physical and spiritual stillness is further emphasized in the concept of Khushu. Khushu involves not just the body but the heart as well. When a believer stands before Allah in prayer, their heart should be humbled, their mind focused, and their body still. The outward stillness, combined with the inner awareness of Allah's presence, creates a profound sense of reverence and awe that transforms the prayer into a deeply spiritual experience.

Stillness in Salah also fosters a sense of discipline and self-control. In our fast-paced world, where everything seems to move at an accelerated pace, it can be challenging to slow down and focus. Salah provides a structured time each day to pause, reflect, and realign ourselves with our ultimate purpose. The deliberate stillness in each movement of Salah trains the believer to be patient, to focus on the present moment, and to resist the urge to rush through important tasks.

This sense of discipline is not limited to Salah alone; it carries over into other aspects of life. When a person learns to control their movements and thoughts in prayer, they are better equipped to exercise patience and mindfulness in their daily interactions and responsibilities. This is one of the many ways in which Salah serves as a means of personal growth and development. The discipline gained from perfecting Salah, particularly through stillness, helps the believer to live a more mindful and balanced life.

Moreover, the act of slowing down and practicing stillness in Salah has a calming effect on the nervous system. It helps to reduce feelings of stress and anxiety, as the rhythmic movements and pauses in prayer bring a sense of order and peace to the mind and body. Salah, when performed with stillness and focus, becomes a refuge from the chaos of the world, offering a time of tranquility and reflection that is essential for maintaining emotional and spiritual well-being.

Reflecting on the broader benefits of stillness in Salah, it becomes clear that this practice is a means of drawing closer to Allah. The physical actions of prayer are more than just movements—they are an expression of the believer's submission, humility, and devotion to their Creator. By performing each action with stillness and concentration, the worshipper shows respect for the sacredness of Salah and for the One whom they are worshipping.

Furthermore, stillness in Salah provides an opportunity for deep spiritual reflection. As the believer stands in prayer, they are reminded of their own fragility and the greatness of Allah. This reflection fosters a sense of gratitude for the countless blessings Allah has bestowed and a desire to live in accordance with His guidance. The moments of stillness in Salah allow for this reflection to take place, making the prayer a time of spiritual nourishment and renewal.

In this way, Salah becomes not just a ritual, but a transformative experience. The act of being still—both physically and mentally—opens the door to deeper spiritual insights and a closer relationship with Allah. This is why the Prophet (PBUH) emphasized the importance of stillness and focus in Salah, urging believers to perfect their prayer in order to reap its full benefits.

Stillness in Salah also helps to cultivate humility, an essential trait for every believer. When a person stands before Allah in prayer, they are reminded of their own limitations and the infinite power of their Creator. This realization naturally leads to a state of humility, where the believer acknowledges their dependence on Allah and seeks His guidance and mercy.

The physical act of bowing and prostrating in Salah reinforces this humility. When the believer lowers themselves to the ground in Sujood, it is a symbolic gesture of submission to Allah's will. The stillness in these positions allows the worshipper to fully internalize the meaning of submission, making the prayer a deeply personal and humbling experience.

This sense of humility carries over into other areas of life. A person who regularly practices stillness and humility in Salah is more likely to approach others with kindness, patience, and understanding. They are less prone to arrogance or pride because they are constantly reminded of their own need for Allah's guidance and mercy. In this way, Salah shapes not only the believer's relationship with Allah but also their interactions with others.

The rewards of stillness in Salah are numerous, both in this life and the Hereafter. In this life, stillness helps to bring about a sense of peace, focus, and discipline that positively impacts all areas of a believer's life. It improves the quality of the prayer itself, making it a time of deep reflection and connection with Allah. It also helps to develop patience and mindfulness, traits that are essential for personal growth and spiritual development.

In the Hereafter, the rewards for those who perfect their Salah are immense. The Prophet Muhammad (PBUH) said, "The first thing a person will be held accountable for on the Day of Judgment is Salah. If it is sound, the rest of their deeds will be sound. If it is lacking, the rest of their deeds will be lacking." This hadith highlights the central importance of Salah in the life of a believer and the need to perform it with excellence.

Achieving stillness in Salah is one of the ways in which a person can ensure that their prayer is sound and acceptable to Allah. By taking the time to perfect each movement and to focus the heart and mind on Allah, the believer fulfills the true purpose of Salah and earns the pleasure of their Creator.

It is important to note that stillness in Salah is not about perfection, but about effort. Every believer, regardless of their level of piety or knowledge, can strive to improve their prayer by focusing on stillness. This effort, no matter how small, is valued by Allah and is a means of drawing closer to Him.

For those who struggle with distractions or impatience in Salah, it is important to remember that improvement takes time. The key is to remain consistent in one's efforts and to seek Allah's help in perfecting the prayer. With persistence and sincerity, stillness in Salah will become easier to achieve, and the benefits of this practice will become more apparent in both the prayer itself and in daily life.

As the believer continues to work on their Salah, they should reflect on the immense blessings that come from this act of worship. Salah is a gift from Allah, a means of purifying the soul, and a way of attaining His mercy and forgiveness. By striving to perfect this gift through stillness, the believer honors the sacredness of prayer and strengthens their bond with Allah.

In conclusion, stillness in Salah is a powerful means of enhancing the quality of one's prayer and deepening the connection with Allah. It involves both physical stillness—ensuring that each movement is performed with care and deliberation—and inner stillness, where the heart and mind are focused solely on worship.

The rewards of stillness are numerous, both in this life and the Hereafter. It brings about a sense of peace, focus, and humility that transforms Salah from a routine task into a deeply spiritual experience. Stillness in Salah also fosters discipline, patience, and mindfulness, traits that are essential for personal and spiritual growth.

Ultimately, stillness in Salah is a reflection of the believer's love and reverence for Allah. It is a way of showing gratitude for the gift of prayer and a means of drawing closer to the Creator. By striving for stillness in Salah, the believer not only perfects their prayer but also enhances their relationship with Allah, leading to a life of greater peace, contentment, and spiritual fulfillment.

10: THE IMPACT OF SALAH ON DAILY LIFE

Salah, the central pillar of Islam, is not just a ritual but a transformative practice that holds the potential to reshape a person's life. When performed with sincerity and humility, Salah acts as a spiritual compass, guiding one towards ethical conduct, patience, and a deeper connection with Allah. It molds the character of a believer, helping to eliminate pride, arrogance, and impatience.

One of the most profound impacts of Salah is the way it fosters a sense of mindfulness in every action throughout the day. By standing in prayer five times a day, a person is constantly reminded of their purpose in life. They remember that their ultimate goal is to please Allah and strive for the hereafter. This constant return to Allah throughout the day, and the deliberate focus on Him, keeps the believer's heart anchored and prevents them from being easily swayed by worldly temptations.

Salah provides an opportunity to pause and reflect. It breaks the monotony of daily activities and grants moments of serenity amidst the chaos of life. Each prayer begins with the call to leave aside worldly engagements and enter a realm of spiritual devotion. The repetitive cycle of bowing, prostrating, and sitting in Salah has a calming effect on the soul, grounding the individual in the present moment. This sense of tranquility extends beyond the prayer, helping a person to approach life's challenges with composure and patience.

The effect of Salah on personal relationships is equally profound. By internalizing the lessons learned in prayer—humility, gratitude, and reliance on Allah—a person can improve their interactions with others. The humility experienced in Sujood (prostration) reminds one of their dependence on Allah and strips away feelings of superiority over others. This humility reflects in how they treat people, fostering kindness and empathy.

Furthermore, the act of prayer helps to cultivate patience. During Salah, a person is required to maintain a calm and steady posture, refraining from hastiness. This patience, learned and practiced in the prayer, spills over into other aspects of life. A person who is patient in Salah finds it easier to remain patient in difficult situations, be it at work, with family, or in the face of personal challenges.

Salah also encourages gratitude. Each time a person stands in prayer, they acknowledge the countless blessings bestowed upon them by Allah. The opening chapter of the Quran, Al-Fatihah, which is recited in every unit of prayer, begins with the words, "All praise is due to Allah, Lord of all the worlds." This constant praise and acknowledgment of Allah's blessings create an attitude of gratitude in the individual, helping them to focus on the positive aspects of life rather than the negative.

The transformative power of Salah is not limited to the individual alone; it extends to the community as well. When believers gather for congregational prayers, a strong sense of unity and brotherhood is fostered. Regardless of one's social or economic status, everyone stands shoulder to shoulder, bowing and prostrating before Allah. This physical alignment symbolizes the equality of all believers and reinforces the concept of Ummah, the global community of Muslims.

In a society where division and inequality often prevail, Salah serves as a reminder that, in the eyes of Allah, all people are equal. This sense of equality nurtured in the mosque or prayer area influences the believer's approach to justice and fairness in their daily interactions. They become more aware of their responsibility to uphold justice and treat others with fairness, regardless of their background or status.

Moreover, Salah reinforces discipline and time management. By establishing a structured routine, where the believer halts their activities to offer Salah at prescribed times, they become more disciplined in their other endeavors. Salah instills the value of time and encourages a balanced life where spiritual duties are given priority. Those who make time for their prayers find it easier to organize their day effectively and fulfill both their religious and worldly responsibilities.

One of the essential aspects of Salah is how it strengthens one's connection to Allah. Each prayer is an intimate conversation between the worshipper and their Creator, where they express their gratitude, seek forgiveness, and ask for guidance. This regular communication fosters a deep sense of trust and reliance on Allah, which carries over into the rest of the day. When faced with trials, a believer who is steadfast in Salah turns to Allah for help, confident in His mercy and wisdom.

This reliance on Allah through Salah leads to increased resilience. Life's challenges, whether they be financial hardships, family issues, or personal struggles, become easier to bear when one trusts in Allah's plan. Salah provides the necessary strength and emotional support, allowing the believer to endure difficulties with a sense of peace and hope.

Salah also acts as a shield against immoral behavior. As mentioned in the Quran, "Verily, Salah restrains one from shameful and unjust deeds" (Surah Al-Ankabut, 29:45). A person who consistently prays with focus and sincerity is less likely to engage in sinful activities. The regular act of bowing before Allah reminds them of their accountability and encourages them to avoid actions that would displease their Creator.

The positive influence of Salah is visible in how it shapes a person's moral compass. A believer who regularly prays becomes more conscious of their actions and is more inclined to engage in righteous behavior. They strive to embody the virtues emphasized in the prayer, such as patience, humility, and gratitude, in their daily lives.

In addition to personal morality, Salah strengthens one's resolve to fulfill social responsibilities. Prayer reminds the believer that they are part of a larger community and that their actions affect others. A person who prays with sincerity will naturally feel a greater sense of responsibility towards their family, neighbors, and society at large. They become more active in charitable efforts, helping the needy, and supporting causes that promote justice and goodness.

Salah also enhances self-discipline. The discipline required to perform Salah at specific times each day builds a strong sense of self-control. This self-discipline extends beyond prayer and helps a person resist temptations, control their emotions, and make better decisions. Whether it's resisting the urge to indulge in sinful behavior or maintaining composure in stressful situations, the self-discipline learned in Salah proves invaluable.

One cannot underestimate the impact of Salah on mental and emotional well-being. In today's fast-paced world, where stress and anxiety have become rampant, Salah offers a much-needed respite. It provides moments of calm and introspection, where the believer can disconnect from worldly concerns and focus solely on their relationship with Allah.

During Salah, the recitation of the Quran, especially verses of hope and comfort, brings peace to the heart. The act of bowing and prostrating also has a therapeutic effect, allowing the individual to release their burdens and submit entirely to the will of Allah. This sense of submission and surrender helps alleviate anxiety and stress, as the believer trusts that Allah is in control of their affairs.

The mindfulness practiced in Salah is akin to modern-day meditation techniques. By focusing on the words of the Quran, the believer trains their mind to stay present and avoid distractions. This practice of mindfulness can help reduce overthinking and increase mental clarity, resulting in a more focused and peaceful state of mind outside of prayer.

The role of Salah in emotional healing is also profound. When a person stands before Allah, they are given the opportunity to pour out their fears, regrets, and hopes. Salah is not merely a mechanical act but an emotional outlet where the believer can seek comfort and guidance. Many find that their burdens feel lighter after a sincere prayer, and this emotional release can have a long-lasting impact on their mental health.

Furthermore, Salah teaches a person how to detach from material concerns and focus on spiritual growth. The world often pushes people towards the pursuit of wealth, status, and pleasure, but Salah pulls the believer back to what truly matters: their relationship with Allah and the pursuit of righteousness. This detachment from worldly desires fosters contentment. A person who is content with their relationship with Allah is less likely to be disturbed by the ups and downs of life.

Additionally, Salah nurtures a strong sense of accountability. Each time a person stands in front of Allah, they are reminded that they will be held accountable for their actions in the hereafter. This constant reminder encourages a believer to live a life that is pleasing to Allah, always mindful of their words and deeds. Knowing that they will be judged on their sincerity, kindness, and fairness instills a sense of responsibility that governs all aspects of their life.

Salah also fosters consistency and perseverance. Regardless of circumstances, whether one is in difficulty or ease, tired or energetic, Salah must be performed. This consistent requirement builds resilience in the believer, teaching them the importance of perseverance. They learn that worship is not contingent on external factors but is a commitment to Allah that transcends all conditions.

This regularity of Salah brings structure and order to a person's life. The fixed times for prayer create a rhythm that breaks the day into manageable parts, allowing the believer to balance work, family, and spiritual obligations. This balance is crucial for maintaining both mental and physical well-being. Instead of becoming overwhelmed by the demands of daily life, the believer finds solace in the predictable nature of Salah and uses it as an anchor to stay grounded.

The practice of making Dua (supplication) within Salah also reinforces a person's connection to Allah. Whether it's in moments of Sujood or during the quiet after prayer, believers are encouraged to make heartfelt Dua. This act of asking Allah for guidance, mercy, or help strengthens their faith and reliance on Him. Through Dua, they acknowledge that only Allah can alleviate their struggles, grant success, or provide peace. This reliance fosters a sense of humility and acceptance, essential traits for personal growth and spiritual success.

Salah plays a significant role in shaping a person's perspective on hardships. Life, by its nature, is full of challenges and tests. However, the believer who is regular in their prayers views these hardships through the lens of divine wisdom. They understand that trials are a means to purify the soul, draw closer to Allah, and earn rewards in the hereafter. This perspective, reinforced through prayer, allows a person to remain steadfast even in the face of adversity.

When faced with difficulties, a person who prays regularly turns to Salah as their refuge. They know that while the world may offer temporary solutions, true peace and relief come from their connection with Allah. By turning to Him in moments of hardship, they strengthen their resolve and build a greater sense of trust in Allah's plan. This trust brings immense peace, as the believer rests assured that whatever happens is by the will of Allah and is ultimately for their benefit, even if it may not be immediately apparent.

Moreover, Salah teaches a person the value of repentance. In every prayer, there is an opportunity to seek forgiveness for past mistakes and sins. The act of consistently turning to Allah, acknowledging one's shortcomings, and asking for forgiveness brings about a sense of renewal and hope. It is through Salah that a believer cleanses their heart and mind from the burdens of guilt, starting each prayer with a fresh commitment to improve.

The element of renewal in Salah is one of its most powerful aspects. Every prayer is an opportunity for a new beginning, where the believer can reflect on their past actions and make a firm intention to do better. The repetitive nature of Salah is not meant to be monotonous but rather a constant reminder that there is always a chance to reform, no matter how many times one may have erred. This sense of continuous renewal instills hope in the believer, preventing them from falling into despair.

Furthermore, the act of Salah is a form of spiritual training. Just as physical exercise strengthens the body, Salah strengthens the soul. Through the disciplined practice of standing, bowing, and prostrating, the believer trains their heart to submit fully to Allah. This submission builds inner strength, resilience, and the ability to resist temptations. The more regularly a person engages in Salah, the stronger their spiritual muscles become, allowing them to face the challenges of life with greater confidence and faith.

Salah also creates a sense of community among Muslims. When performed in congregation, especially during the Jumu'ah (Friday) prayer or Taraweeh during Ramadan, believers come together, united in their worship of Allah. This unity reinforces the idea that they are part of a greater Ummah, bound by their faith and shared devotion. The sense of brotherhood and sisterhood fostered in congregational Salah can be a powerful source of support, helping individuals feel connected and cared for within the Muslim community.

In addition to fostering a sense of community, congregational Salah serves as a reminder of the collective responsibility Muslims have towards one another. When a person stands beside their fellow worshippers, they are reminded that they are part of something larger than themselves. This sense of belonging encourages empathy and concern for others, motivating the believer to help those in need and to contribute positively to society.

The collective nature of Salah also teaches equality. Regardless of wealth, status, or background, every believer stands in the same rows, bowing and prostrating before Allah. This sense of equality reinforces the idea that in the eyes of Allah, what matters is a person's piety and sincerity, not their worldly achievements. This understanding humbles the believer and inspires them to treat others with kindness and respect, regardless of their position in society.

Moreover, Salah serves as a reminder of the transient nature of this world. Each prayer, especially the five daily prayers, is a reminder that life is temporary and that the true home of the believer is in the hereafter. This awareness encourages a person to focus on their spiritual goals rather than getting caught up in the material pursuits of this world. The regular practice of Salah helps keep the heart detached from the fleeting pleasures of the dunya (world) and focused on what truly matters—the pleasure of Allah and the eternal rewards of the afterlife.

The spiritual detachment cultivated through Salah does not mean that a person neglects their worldly duties. On the contrary, Salah enhances a person's ability to perform their responsibilities with excellence and integrity. By constantly reminding the believer of their purpose, Salah motivates them to fulfill their roles—whether as a parent, spouse, employee, or friend—with sincerity and dedication. Knowing that their actions are being observed by Allah pushes the believer to excel in all areas of life, always striving to maintain high standards of honesty, fairness, and compassion.

Salah also instills a deep sense of gratitude. Every time a person prays, they are reminded of the countless blessings that Allah has bestowed upon them. From the simple act of being able to breathe to the larger blessings of health, family, and sustenance, Salah encourages the believer to reflect on these favors. This reflection fosters a spirit of gratitude, which in turn brings contentment and peace. A person who is grateful to Allah for their blessings is less likely to feel envious or dissatisfied with their circumstances, as they recognize that everything they have is a gift from their Creator.

Another crucial benefit of Salah is its ability to inspire self-improvement. Each prayer is a chance to assess one's spiritual state and make the necessary adjustments to become a better Muslim. Whether it's improving one's character, increasing acts of worship, or seeking knowledge, Salah encourages continuous growth. The regular act of turning to Allah throughout the day reminds the believer that there is always room for improvement, and that no matter how much they progress, there is always more to achieve in their spiritual journey.

In addition to self-improvement, Salah instills in a believer the importance of humility. Each time a person bows down in Ruku or prostrates in Sujood, they are physically manifesting their submission to Allah. These postures are symbolic acts of surrender, reminding the believer that no matter how much they achieve in life, they are still dependent on Allah for everything. This humility is central to the Islamic character, as it teaches the believer to live a life free from arrogance and self-importance. The more one performs Salah, the more they are reminded of their own limitations and of Allah's infinite power.

Humility in Salah is not just limited to the physical acts of bowing and prostrating; it extends to the heart as well. A humble heart in Salah is one that acknowledges its flaws, weaknesses, and need for Allah's mercy. This inner humility brings about a state of Khushu (deep concentration and humility), which is essential for the acceptance of the prayer. A heart that is filled with arrogance or heedlessness cannot truly connect with Allah during Salah. Therefore, each prayer is an opportunity to purify the heart from pride and to replace it with sincere humility before the Creator.

Furthermore, Salah teaches a person to have patience and perseverance. There are moments when a person may not feel the spiritual upliftment they desire during prayer. Despite this, they are required to continue with their prayers, trusting that Allah will reward their persistence. This practice of continuing even when the heart feels distant is a lesson in patience, reminding the believer that success, whether in this world or the next, often requires consistent effort and trust in Allah's timing.

Patience in Salah also teaches the believer to maintain hope. Even in the most difficult times, when it seems as though life is overwhelming, Salah reminds the believer that Allah is always near. The mere act of raising one's hands in Dua or prostrating in submission is a powerful reminder that Allah is aware of all their struggles and that relief will come, either in this life or the next. This hope is what keeps many believers steadfast in their prayers, knowing that their efforts are not in vain.

In a broader sense, the discipline learned through Salah extends to other areas of life. A person who can consistently commit to their prayers is likely to develop discipline in other aspects of their life, whether it be in their work, family responsibilities, or personal goals. Salah acts as a daily reminder of the importance of time management and dedication. This discipline is a key factor in achieving success in all areas of life, as it teaches a person to be consistent, focused, and mindful of their actions.

Moreover, the act of regularly communicating with Allah through Salah strengthens a person's connection to their Creator. This connection brings about a sense of purpose and fulfillment that cannot be found in material pursuits. It reassures the believer that no matter how alone they may feel in the world, they are never truly alone as long as they have their connection with Allah. This sense of companionship with the Creator brings about peace and contentment, allowing the believer to navigate life's challenges with confidence and calmness.

In addition to fostering a deep connection with Allah, Salah serves as a continuous reminder of a person's ultimate goal: the hereafter. Every act of worship, especially Salah, is a means of preparing for the day when the believer will stand before Allah and be held accountable for their deeds. This reminder motivates the believer to live a life of righteousness, striving to accumulate good deeds and avoid actions that displease Allah. The constant focus on the hereafter instills a sense of responsibility, encouraging the believer to prioritize what truly matters.

Salah also provides an opportunity for self-reflection. With each prayer, the believer is given a moment to pause and evaluate their actions, intentions, and spiritual state. This regular self-assessment is crucial for personal growth. It allows the believer to identify their weaknesses, seek forgiveness for their mistakes, and make a sincere intention to improve. The opportunity for renewal that comes with each prayer is a mercy from Allah, giving the believer a fresh start throughout the day.

Through Salah, a person also gains a sense of peace and tranquility. In a world filled with distractions and stress, the few moments spent in Salah offer a time of stillness and reflection. The rhythmic nature of the prayer, combined with the focus on Allah, calms the mind and soothes the soul. This inner peace is one of the most profound benefits of Salah, as it provides the believer with a sense of serenity that transcends the chaos of the outside world.

This tranquility achieved through Salah has a profound effect on a person's overall well-being. Studies have shown that regular prayer can reduce stress, anxiety, and depression. The act of turning to Allah in worship and supplication helps a person release their worries and trust in Allah's plan. This trust alleviates the psychological burden of trying to control every aspect of life, bringing about a sense of ease and acceptance. By recognizing that ultimate control lies with Allah, the believer can let go of the need to micromanage their life and instead focus on doing their best while leaving the results to Allah.

Another benefit of Salah is the sense of humility it cultivates towards others. A person who regularly prays is reminded of their own dependence on Allah, which in turn makes them more compassionate and understanding towards others. This humility prevents them from looking down on those who may be struggling or less fortunate. Instead, the believer is encouraged to offer help, support, and kindness to others, knowing that all humans are equal in the eyes of Allah and that true superiority lies in piety and good character, not in wealth or status.

Moreover, Salah teaches the believer the importance of gratitude. Every prayer begins with the phrase "Alhamdulillah," meaning "All praise is due to Allah." This constant reminder of Allah's blessings encourages the believer to reflect on the many gifts they have been given, from health to family to sustenance. By regularly expressing gratitude through Salah, the believer nurtures a positive outlook on life, focusing on what they have rather than what they lack. This attitude of gratitude is not only pleasing to Allah but also has a positive effect on the believer's mental and emotional well-being.

Gratitude cultivated through Salah also has a ripple effect on the way a person interacts with others. When a person is grateful for their own blessings, they are less likely to envy others or to harbor feelings of resentment. Instead, they are more inclined to appreciate the success and happiness of others, fostering positive relationships and a sense of community. This attitude of contentment and gratitude brings about a sense of harmony both within the individual and in their interactions with others.

Salah also fosters mindfulness, a state of being fully present in the moment. During prayer, the believer is required to focus on their recitations, movements, and connection to Allah. This practice of mindfulness, when carried over into other aspects of life, helps the believer become more aware of their thoughts, actions, and surroundings. It encourages them to live with intentionality, making conscious decisions that align with their values and beliefs. This heightened sense of awareness improves the quality of life, as the believer is no longer acting on autopilot but is fully engaged in every moment. Furthermore, Salah teaches the believer to rely on Allah's guidance in all matters. By regularly seeking Allah's help through prayer and supplication, the believer acknowledges that their own knowledge and abilities are limited. They turn to Allah, who is Al-Hakeem (The Wise) and Al-Aleem (The All-Knowing), trusting that He will guide them to what is best. This reliance on Allah brings about a sense of security, as the believer knows that they are not alone in making decisions or facing challenges. This trust in Allah's wisdom and plan brings immense comfort and allows the believer to navigate life's uncertainties with confidence and faith.

Salah also teaches accountability. By regularly standing before Allah in prayer, the believer is reminded that they will one day stand before Him in the hereafter to account for their deeds. This awareness of accountability fosters a sense of responsibility, pushing the believer to strive for righteousness and avoid actions that displease Allah. The constant reminder of the Day of Judgment helps the believer stay on the straight path, as they know that their every word and action is being recorded and will be weighed on the scales of justice.

In addition to accountability, Salah fosters resilience. Life is full of trials, tests, and hardships, but Salah provides the believer with the spiritual strength needed to endure them. Through regular communication with Allah, the believer builds a reservoir of inner strength that allows them to face difficulties with patience and trust in Allah's plan. This resilience is not just about enduring hardships but about emerging from them stronger and more spiritually connected to Allah.

The act of Salah also deepens a believer's sense of Tawakkul, or trust in Allah. By consistently turning to Allah in prayer, the believer develops a deep sense of reliance on His wisdom and mercy. This trust alleviates much of the stress and anxiety that comes with uncertainty, as the believer knows that whatever happens is by Allah's decree and is ultimately for their benefit. This sense of trust brings about peace, as the believer no longer feels the need to control every outcome but instead focuses on fulfilling their responsibilities while leaving the results to Allah.

In addition to fostering trust in Allah, Salah serves as a constant reminder of the importance of repentance. Each prayer offers the believer an opportunity to seek forgiveness for their sins and shortcomings. The act of regularly asking Allah for forgiveness fosters a sense of humility and self-awareness. It reminds the believer that they are not perfect and that they need Allah's mercy and guidance to stay on the right path. This practice of repentance prevents the heart from becoming hardened by sin and keeps the believer in a state of spiritual purity.

The emphasis on repentance in Salah also brings about a sense of renewal. With each prayer, the believer has the chance to start fresh, leaving behind past mistakes and moving forward with a renewed commitment to righteousness. This sense of renewal is a powerful motivator, as it encourages the believer to continuously strive for improvement, knowing that no matter how many times they may have fallen short, Allah's mercy is always available to those who seek it sincerely.

Finally, Salah serves as a reminder of the ultimate reality: the hereafter. Each time the believer prays, they are reminded that this world is temporary and that their ultimate destination is either Jannah (paradise) or Jahannam (hellfire). This constant focus on the hereafter encourages the believer to prioritize their spiritual goals over their worldly desires. It motivates them to work towards earning Allah's pleasure and avoiding actions that lead to His displeasure. This focus on the hereafter is a guiding force in the believer's life, helping them make decisions that are aligned with their faith and their ultimate goal of attaining eternal success in the hereafter.

Through the practice of Salah, the believer is given the tools to navigate life's challenges, cultivate inner peace, and maintain a strong connection with Allah. Each prayer is an opportunity for self-reflection, growth, and renewal. It is a reminder of the believer's purpose, their reliance on Allah, and their ultimate goal in the hereafter. The benefits of Salah extend far beyond the physical act of worship; they shape the believer's character, mindset, and approach to life. Salah teaches the believer the value of discipline, patience, gratitude, and humility. It fosters a deep sense of accountability, reminding the believer that they will one day stand before Allah to answer for their deeds. It also provides a sense of peace and comfort, as the believer knows that Allah is always near, listening to their supplications and guiding them through life's trials. Through Salah, the believer is constantly reminded of their ultimate purpose: to worship Allah and strive for success in the hereafter.

11: OVERCOMING DISTRACTIONS IN SALAH

In the heart of Salah lies a special treasure that every believer longs to attain—Khushu. The essence of Khushu is more than just focus; it is a deep emotional and spiritual connection to the act of worship, where the heart and mind are entirely immersed in remembering Allah, leaving behind the distractions of the world. However, attaining this profound state is often easier said than done. One of the greatest struggles during prayer is to overcome the countless distractions that pull us away from experiencing Khushu.

Worldly thoughts, concerns about daily responsibilities, and even anxieties of the future can cloud the mind in Salah. The first step in addressing distractions in Salah is to recognize their source. Distractions stem from two places: external factors and internal disturbances. External factors include the surroundings, noise, or even other people praying nearby. Internal disturbances are often more challenging to control—they arise from the whisperings of Shaytan, worries about worldly affairs, or a restless heart.

Recognizing the cause of these distractions is essential to overcoming them.

The Qur'an and the Sunnah provide a comprehensive understanding of how to attain tranquility and focus during Salah. By implementing the wisdom contained in these sources, one can effectively guard against distractions and connect fully with Allah in prayer.

The Prophet Muhammad (peace be upon him) warned us about the dangers of neglecting focus in Salah. One of the key elements that separate a heartfelt Salah from a ritualistic one is the level of attention given during the act. The famous verse in the Qur'an, **"Indeed, the believers have succeeded. Those who during their prayers are humbly submissive"** (Al-Mu'minun: 1-2), highlights the value of Khushu and how it is linked directly to success in this world and the Hereafter. Being heedless in prayer can lead to it becoming a mere physical exercise, devoid of spiritual nourishment.

One effective strategy to cultivate focus and guard against distractions is to prepare mentally before the prayer. Before beginning Salah, take a moment to quiet the mind and focus on the act of standing before Allah. Remind yourself that this is not just a ritual but a moment of intimate conversation with the Creator. The Prophet (peace be upon him) used to say before his Salah: **"Establish the prayer as if it is your final one."** This simple shift in mindset helps clear away unnecessary thoughts and prioritizes the present moment, making the experience of Salah much more profound.

A common struggle during Salah is the wandering mind, which may shift between thoughts about work, family, or other personal concerns. To combat this, one should reflect on the verses being recited. When you focus on the meanings of the Qur'an, it helps redirect your thoughts to the prayer itself, leaving little room for external distractions.

An essential element in overcoming distractions during Salah is to ensure the place of prayer is conducive to focus. The environment plays a significant role in one's ability to concentrate. A cluttered, noisy, or distracting space can make it difficult to maintain Khushu. The Prophet (peace be upon him) emphasized the importance of finding a peaceful, clean space for prayer. It is reported in several Hadiths that even a simple object, such as a curtain with distracting patterns, was removed to help maintain focus during prayer. Ensuring that your prayer space is calm and free from unnecessary distractions helps set the tone for a mindful Salah.

Another important factor is your own physical state before Salah. Tiredness, hunger, or stress can all contribute to a wandering mind. The Prophet (peace be upon him) advised believers to eat or rest if necessary before performing prayer to avoid being preoccupied with those needs during worship. Ensuring that both body and mind are prepared for the act of prayer is crucial to overcoming distractions.

When it comes to internal distractions, the whisperings of Shaytan often play a role. Shaytan's goal is to divert our attention from the remembrance of

Allah. He tries to fill our minds with irrelevant thoughts to diminish the rewards of Salah. The Prophet (peace be upon him) taught us to seek refuge in Allah from these whisperings by saying: **"I seek refuge with Allah from the accursed Shaytan"** before beginning the prayer. This invocation acts as a shield against the distractions that arise from external or internal influences.

The Prophet Muhammad (peace be upon him) demonstrated how a believer can achieve a state of tranquility and Khushu in Salah by emphasizing stillness in each posture. When a person moves too quickly in Salah, rushing through the motions without giving time for reflection and calmness, it is much easier for the mind to wander. The Prophet (peace be upon him) advised us to perform each action of Salah with deliberate care, ensuring that the heart and mind are engaged with the prayer. He said, **"The worst thief is the one who steals from his prayer."** When asked how a person can steal from their prayer, he responded, **"By not performing the Ruku' and Sujood properly."**

Maintaining physical stillness in Salah helps to create a mental stillness that enhances focus. Each movement, whether it is bowing, standing, or prostrating, should be performed with purpose. Pausing for a moment in each position to reflect on the act itself, and what it represents, can significantly deepen one's connection to the prayer and reduce distractions.

In addition to physical stillness, it is important to engage the heart in the prayer. One practical method is to imagine that you are standing directly before Allah. The Prophet (peace be upon him) taught that when you pray, you should pray as though you can see Allah, and if you cannot, then at least believe that He is watching you. This conscious awareness of Allah's presence makes it much more difficult for the mind to stray towards worldly distractions.

Another effective strategy to combat distractions during Salah is by cultivating a deeper understanding of the meanings behind the words being recited. Many times, distractions arise because the person praying is not fully engaged with the recitation. By learning the meanings of the Surahs, particularly Surah Al-Fatihah, and reflecting on their significance, one can immerse themselves more in the prayer.

For example, when reciting **"Alhamdulillahi Rabbil 'Alamin"** (All praise is due to Allah, the Lord of all worlds), take a moment to reflect on what it means for Allah to be the sustainer of the entire universe. Understanding the depth of these words helps to bring the mind back to the prayer and focuses it on the majesty of Allah. Similarly, when saying **"You alone we worship, and You alone we ask for help"** (Surah Al-Fatihah, Ayah 5), let the heart absorb the meaning of relying solely on Allah for guidance and assistance. This approach helps anchor the mind in the prayer itself, preventing it from wandering towards external thoughts.

Using the tools of reflection, stillness, and understanding the meanings of the Qur'an can help ensure a more focused and sincere Salah. Each prayer is an opportunity to not just fulfill a religious obligation, but to strengthen the connection with Allah, deepen the faith, and build a relationship of trust and devotion.

Overcoming distractions in Salah is a journey, one that requires patience, practice, and persistence. Shaytan will continue to try to interrupt your focus, but through constant effort and reliance on Allah, it is possible to improve the quality of your prayer. Seeking Allah's help in overcoming distractions is key. The Prophet Muhammad (peace be upon him) taught us to frequently recite the supplication, **"O Allah, help me in remembering You, thanking You, and worshipping You in the best manner."** This Du'a not only helps us focus on the act of worship but also brings blessings into our lives, ensuring that Allah is with us in our efforts to offer sincere and focused prayers.

Developing a sense of mindfulness in Salah requires an understanding that prayer is not a hurried obligation but a moment of peace, reflection, and spiritual renewal. One of the most effective ways to deepen the experience of Salah is to approach it with a mindset of gratitude. Gratitude opens the heart to the blessings bestowed by Allah, and when this gratitude is reflected in prayer, distractions are minimized. When you stand in prayer, take a moment to remember the countless blessings Allah has granted—health, sustenance, safety, and, above all, the gift of Islam.

Gratitude has a powerful ability to center the mind and heart. As you begin Salah, reflect on the opportunity to connect with Allah. Recognizing prayer as a gift rather than a duty allows the individual to approach it with a sense of joy and anticipation. When the heart is full of gratitude, it is less likely to be distracted by worldly concerns. This shift in mindset transforms Salah from a routine task into a cherished moment of spiritual connection.

Engaging the heart in gratitude helps anchor the believer in the present moment. The Prophet (peace be upon him) emphasized the importance of presence in Salah, not just in body, but in spirit. He stated, **"When one of you prays, he is speaking privately with his Lord."** Keeping this in mind helps remind the worshipper of the intimacy of the prayer, encouraging them to give their full attention to the conversation with Allah.

One of the most common complaints regarding distractions in Salah is the racing of thoughts about the future or the past. During prayer, it is easy to get caught up thinking about tasks that need to be done or revisiting events from the past. To combat this, one must train the mind to live in the present moment. Salah is the ideal opportunity to practice mindfulness, where the focus is on the now, rather than the past or the future.

The Qur'an encourages this practice by reminding believers of the fleeting nature of worldly life. In Surah Al-Asr, Allah says, **"By time, indeed mankind is in loss, except for those who have believed and done righteous deeds and advised each other to truth and advised each other to patience."** This verse highlights the importance of time and how we must use it wisely, particularly in our acts of worship. Reflecting on the limited nature of time helps believers prioritize their Salah and remain focused throughout the prayer, avoiding the tendency to let their minds drift into the future or the past.

Incorporating deep, reflective breathing into Salah is another practical tool to maintain focus. Slow, deliberate breaths can help calm the mind and bring it back to the present. The Prophet (peace be upon him) would often take deep breaths during his moments of contemplation, helping him focus on the enormity of standing before Allah. By consciously controlling one's breathing during prayer, the believer can eliminate tension and stress, creating a more tranquil environment for worship.

Another essential aspect of overcoming distractions in Salah is acknowledging that achieving perfect focus is a gradual process. The path to attaining Khushu in prayer is not always linear, and it requires consistent effort. The companion of the Prophet, Hudhayfah Ibn Al-Yaman (may Allah be pleased with him), said, **"The first thing you will lose of your religion is Khushu, and the last thing you will lose of your religion is the prayer. There may be no Khushu in the hearts of people, and they will be performing the prayer."**

This profound statement serves as a reminder that while maintaining focus in Salah is crucial, the process of developing Khushu is a journey that will have its ups and downs. A key part of this journey is seeking Allah's assistance in maintaining focus. One of the most beautiful and powerful du'as (supplications) that the Prophet (peace be upon him) would often recite was: **"O Allah, I seek refuge in You from knowledge that does not benefit, from a heart that is not humble, from a soul that is not satisfied, and from a supplication that is not answered."** This du'a reflects the importance of having a humble heart in prayer and a soul that is content with the remembrance of Allah.

A practical step to maintaining focus and overcoming distractions is to remember death. The Prophet (peace be upon him) encouraged us to pray as though it were our last prayer. This mindset helps to strip away the unnecessary clutter from our thoughts, reminding us of the brevity of life and the urgency of making each prayer meaningful. **"Remember often the destroyer of pleasures (death),"** he advised, as this helps put the trials and distractions of daily life into perspective, allowing the worshipper to focus on what truly matters—connecting with Allah.

The importance of proper posture and movements in Salah cannot be overstated. Rushing through the actions of prayer can often lead to a lack of focus and an increase in distractions. The Prophet (peace be upon him) emphasized performing each movement with deliberation and care. He said, **"The worst thief is the one who steals from his prayer."** When asked how this could happen, he replied, **"By not completing its bowing and prostration properly."**

This Hadith serves as a reminder that each movement in Salah should be given its due right. Rushing through the bowing (Ruku) or prostration (Sujood) can diminish the overall quality of the prayer. The bowing is not merely an act of bending; it is a symbol of submission to Allah, where the believer humbles themselves before their Creator. Similarly, prostration is the closest a servant comes to their Lord, as mentioned by the Prophet (peace be upon him). Performing these actions with care and awareness helps to create a flow in Salah, where each movement transitions smoothly into the next, enhancing focus and minimizing distractions.

One practical tip is to focus on the sensations during these postures. When in Ruku, reflect on the weight of your body bending before Allah. In Sujood, take a moment to feel the humility of placing your forehead on the ground, acknowledging your complete dependence on Allah. These physical reflections help to anchor the mind in the present, reducing the tendency to be distracted by external or internal thoughts.

It is vital to remember that Salah is not merely a set of physical actions, but an act of devotion that involves the heart, mind, and soul. The internal state of the worshipper plays a crucial role in the quality of their prayer. One of the most effective ways to elevate the internal state is through the regular remembrance of Allah (Dhikr) outside of Salah. The more a person remembers Allah throughout the day, the easier it becomes to remain focused during prayer. The Prophet (peace be upon him) said, **"The example of the one who remembers Allah and the one who does not is like that of the living and the dead."**

Engaging in regular Dhikr helps to create a heart that is constantly aware of Allah, making it easier to focus during Salah. When the heart is accustomed to remembering Allah throughout the day, distractions become less prominent in prayer. This practice softens the heart and allows the believer to enter Salah with a mind already attuned to worship.

The Qur'an also emphasizes the importance of Dhikr in creating a heart that is free from distractions. **"Indeed, in the remembrance of Allah do hearts find rest"** (Surah Ar-Ra'd: 28). By incorporating Dhikr into daily routines, whether through reciting specific supplications, reflecting on Allah's creation, or engaging in quiet moments of contemplation, one prepares the heart for Salah. This constant state of mindfulness outside of prayer enhances the ability to focus during the act of worship, ensuring a more fulfilling and spiritually enriching experience.

A key aspect of maintaining focus in Salah is understanding the meanings of the words and actions performed during prayer. Often, distractions arise because the mind wanders when the individual lacks a deep understanding of what they are reciting. To combat this, it is essential to study the meanings of the Surahs and supplications recited in Salah. When a person fully comprehends the words of Surah Al-Fatiha, the significance of each verse resonates deeply within their heart, making it less likely for their thoughts to stray.

Take, for instance, the opening verse, **"Alhamdulillahi Rabbil 'Aalameen"** (All praise is due to Allah, the Lord of all the worlds). By reflecting on the majesty and dominion of Allah, the worshipper is reminded that their entire existence is owed to the Creator. Similarly, when one recites, **"Iyyaka na'budu wa iyyaka nasta'een"** (You alone we worship, and You alone we ask for help), they reaffirm their complete dependence on Allah for guidance and assistance. Understanding these meanings creates a deeper connection with the prayer, allowing the worshipper to feel each word and verse instead of simply reciting them mechanically.

Another practical step is to focus on the transitions between different postures in Salah. Each movement carries a specific meaning and helps the worshipper to focus on their state of submission to Allah. For example, the bowing (Ruku) symbolizes the humbling of oneself before the majesty of Allah, and the prostration (Sujood) represents the highest form of submission and closeness to the Creator. When a person understands these symbolic meanings, they are more likely to maintain focus throughout the prayer.

Distractions in Salah are not only mental but can also arise from external factors. Creating a conducive environment for prayer is essential for minimizing these distractions. The Prophet (peace be upon him) recommended that places of prayer be kept clean, simple, and free from distractions. He said, **"Pray as you have seen me praying."** Part of this instruction includes ensuring that the prayer space is free from objects or noises that may cause the mind to wander.

One effective way to create a peaceful environment is to establish a specific place in the home dedicated to Salah. This space should be free from clutter and distractions, allowing the individual to enter into a state of peace and focus as soon as they begin praying. Additionally, performing Salah in a clean and serene environment reflects the sunnah of the Prophet (peace be upon him), who placed great emphasis on cleanliness in all aspects of life, including worship. Keeping the prayer space tidy and removing unnecessary items from sight can help create a more focused atmosphere, reducing external distractions.

Dressing appropriately for Salah also plays a role in maintaining focus. Wearing clean, modest clothing that is free from intricate designs or distractions allows the worshipper to focus solely on their connection with Allah. The Prophet (peace be upon him) once noticed a man praying in a garment that had distracting designs, and he instructed the man to wear simpler clothing. This underscores the importance of minimizing distractions both in the environment and in personal attire to ensure that the mind remains focused on the prayer.

In addition to external preparations, internal preparation is equally important for maintaining focus in Salah. One of the most powerful ways to prepare internally is by performing the Sunnah prayers before the obligatory Salah. These Sunnah prayers act as a spiritual warm-up, helping the believer to transition from the distractions of daily life into a state of mindfulness. The Prophet (peace be upon him) consistently offered Sunnah prayers, and he encouraged his companions to do the same. These voluntary prayers are an opportunity to perfect one's Khushu (focus) and devotion before engaging in the obligatory acts of worship.

The Sunnah prayers allow the worshipper to practice concentration and mindfulness in a more relaxed setting, as there is less pressure to complete the prayer perfectly. By the time the obligatory prayer begins, the individual is already in a heightened state of focus, having set aside the concerns of daily life. In this way, the Sunnah prayers serve as a buffer that shields the worshipper from distractions and prepares the heart and mind for the main act of worship.

Another internal preparation that enhances focus is performing Wudu (ablution) with mindfulness. The Prophet (peace be upon him) taught that Wudu is not only a physical cleansing but also a spiritual purification. When performed with the intention of cleansing both the body and the soul, Wudu helps prepare the believer for a more meaningful connection with Allah. As each part of the body is washed, the individual should reflect on the significance of purifying oneself for the purpose of standing before the Creator. This reflection creates a sense of reverence and readiness for Salah, making it easier to maintain focus during the prayer itself.

Beyond the physical and mental preparations, seeking refuge in Allah from distractions is an essential part of ensuring focus in Salah. The Prophet (peace be upon him) advised his companions to seek Allah's protection from the whispers of Shaytan (Satan), who constantly tries to distract the worshipper during prayer. He taught them to say, **"I seek refuge with Allah from the accursed Shaytan,"** before beginning Salah. This simple yet powerful invocation acts as a spiritual shield, blocking the attempts of Shaytan to interfere with the worshipper's connection with Allah.

It is important to remember that distractions during prayer are often a test of patience and focus. Shaytan's primary goal is to divert the believer's attention away from their worship, and he uses various tactics to achieve this. By acknowledging the presence of distractions and turning to Allah for help, the worshipper can overcome these obstacles and maintain their focus. The Prophet (peace be upon him) also recommended making Dhikr (remembrance of Allah) after prayer as a way to fortify the heart and protect it from further distractions. By consistently seeking Allah's help, the believer is empowered to resist distractions and maintain a stronger connection in Salah.

The Qur'an reinforces this concept of seeking refuge from Shaytan's whispers, as mentioned in Surah Al-A'raf, **"And if an evil suggestion comes to you from Shaytan, then seek refuge in Allah. Indeed, He is Hearing and Knowing."** This verse reminds the believer that Allah is always present, ready to assist those who seek His help in overcoming distractions and maintaining focus in their acts of worship. It encourages reliance on Allah's protection to safeguard the sanctity of the prayer.

Another strategy for overcoming distractions is to engage the senses during prayer. By paying attention to the physical sensations of Salah—the feeling of the ground beneath one's feet, the sound of the Takbeer (saying Allahu Akbar), and the rhythm of the breath—worshippers can anchor themselves in the present moment. Engaging the senses helps to bring the mind back to the prayer whenever it begins to wander. This technique is particularly useful for those who struggle with mental distractions, as it provides a tangible way to reconnect with the act of worship.

The Prophet (peace be upon him) was known to engage his senses fully during Salah. He would pray with such mindfulness that his companions could hear his heart beating, and his tears would flow freely when he reflected on the mercy of Allah. This level of emotional and physical engagement in Salah is something every believer should strive for. By becoming more aware of the sensations in their body and surroundings, the worshipper creates a stronger connection between their physical actions and their spiritual intentions.

Additionally, engaging the senses helps the individual to become more attuned to the rhythm of the prayer. Each movement in Salah has a unique tempo, from the Takbeer to the bowing and prostration. When the worshipper focuses on these movements, they can create a natural flow in the prayer, minimizing the opportunity for distractions to take root. This rhythm not only enhances the quality of the prayer but also deepens the spiritual experience, allowing the individual to feel more connected to Allah.

One of the ultimate goals of overcoming distractions in Salah is to develop a state of deep contemplation and reflection on Allah's greatness. This state, known as **Tafakkur**, is highly encouraged in Islam as it leads to a more profound understanding of one's relationship with the Creator. Tafakkur involves reflecting on the attributes of Allah—His mercy, His power, His wisdom—and how these attributes manifest in the life of the believer.

During Salah, Tafakkur can be achieved by contemplating the meanings of the verses being recited. For instance, when reciting **"Maliki yawmid-Deen"** (Master of the Day of Judgment), the worshipper should reflect on the reality of the Day of Judgment and how their actions in this life will be weighed on that day. By internalizing the meaning of the verses, the worshipper elevates their prayer from a mere physical ritual to a deeply spiritual experience.

Tafakkur also involves reflecting on the beauty and intricacy of Allah's creation. When a believer stands in Salah, they should remember that they are part of the vast universe created by Allah, who sustains everything with His will. This reflection fosters a sense of humility and awe, making it easier to focus during prayer. The Prophet (peace be upon him) encouraged Tafakkur as a way to deepen one's connection with Allah, stating, **"An hour of reflection is better than a year of worship."** This highlights the importance of mindful reflection in achieving true focus in Salah.

A crucial aspect of maintaining concentration in Salah is the intention (**Niyyah**) behind the prayer. The sincerity of one's intention plays a significant role in the quality of their prayer. Before beginning Salah, it is important to consciously remind oneself of the purpose behind the prayer. One should reflect on their need for Allah's guidance, forgiveness, and blessings, rather than treating Salah as a mere obligation.

The Prophet Muhammad (peace be upon him) emphasized the importance of intention, saying, **"Actions are judged by intentions, and every person will get what they intended."** This hadith serves as a powerful reminder that the quality of one's actions, including Salah, is determined by the sincerity and purpose behind them. When a worshipper consciously sets the intention to seek closeness to Allah through prayer, they are more likely to remain focused and engaged throughout the Salah.

In addition to setting a clear intention, it is also beneficial to visualize standing before Allah. By reminding oneself that they are in the presence of the Almighty, the worshipper can create a sense of awe and reverence that enhances their focus. This visualization strengthens the connection between the physical act of Salah and the spiritual objective of seeking Allah's pleasure. The more consistently a person practices this, the more naturally their focus will align with their intention.

Another method of enhancing focus in Salah is to lengthen the time spent in each posture. Many people rush through the actions of Salah, moving quickly from one posture to the next without taking the time to reflect. However, slowing down and allowing oneself to fully experience each position helps to cultivate a sense of mindfulness. The Prophet Muhammad (peace be upon him) advised his followers to perform Salah with calmness and deliberation, as this allows the worshipper to fully engage in the prayer both mentally and physically.

During Ruku (bowing), for example, the believer should take time to reflect on the glory of Allah, as symbolized by the act of bowing in submission. Saying **"Subhana Rabbiyal Azeem"** (Glory is to my Lord, the Most Great) three times with full concentration and sincerity deepens the sense of humility. Similarly, during Sujood (prostration), it is important to stay in that position long enough to feel the full impact of this act of worship. Sujood is the moment when the worshipper is closest to Allah, and by prolonging this posture, one strengthens their spiritual connection and creates a profound sense of closeness to the Creator.

It is also beneficial to lengthen the recitation of the Quran during Salah. The Prophet (peace be upon him) would often recite long portions of the Quran in his prayers, especially during Tahajjud (the night prayer). Reciting longer Surahs with understanding and reflection creates more time for contemplation and minimizes the likelihood of the mind wandering. By making this a regular practice, the worshipper not only enhances their concentration but also deepens their relationship with the Quran.

Developing mindfulness in Salah requires consistent practice and effort. One effective way to train the mind to focus is to engage in **Dhikr** (remembrance of Allah) outside of prayer. Dhikr helps to cleanse the heart and align the soul with the remembrance of Allah, making it easier to maintain focus during Salah. The Prophet (peace be upon him) encouraged his companions to engage in Dhikr regularly, saying, **"Shall I not tell you of the best of your deeds, the purest of them with your Lord, and the highest of them in your ranks, and better for you than spending gold and silver, and better for you than meeting your enemy and striking their necks and they striking your necks?"** They said, 'Yes, O Messenger of Allah.' He said, 'The remembrance of Allah.'" This hadith highlights the immense value of Dhikr in purifying the heart and maintaining a constant awareness of Allah.

Incorporating Dhikr into daily life creates a habit of mindfulness that extends into Salah. By frequently reciting phrases such as **"SubhanAllah"** (Glory be to Allah), **"Alhamdulillah"** (All praise is due to Allah), and **"Allahu Akbar"** (Allah is the Greatest), the believer strengthens their connection with Allah. This practice helps to keep the heart focused on Allah even outside of formal prayer, which in turn makes it easier to remain concentrated during Salah.

Furthermore, Dhikr can be a powerful tool for overcoming worldly distractions. When a person faces stress, anxiety, or overwhelming thoughts, engaging in the remembrance of Allah serves as a means of calming the mind and centering the soul. This mental clarity translates into a more focused and serene state during prayer. By making Dhikr a regular part of one's routine, the believer gradually trains their mind to avoid distractions, not only during Salah but throughout the day.

12: **ATTAINING CONSISTENCY IN KHUSHU**

Attaining consistency in Khushu (focus and humility) during Salah is one of the most rewarding spiritual achievements for a Muslim. Khushu is not a one-time experience; it is an ongoing journey that requires discipline, reflection, and dedication. Developing and maintaining a state of Khushu ensures that each prayer brings the worshipper closer to Allah and enriches the soul.

However, maintaining Khushu consistently can be challenging due to the constant distractions and temptations that exist in daily life.

The key to attaining consistency in Khushu is rooted in intention and preparation. Before entering the prayer, the mind and heart must be free from worldly concerns. The moments leading up to the prayer can set the tone for the entire act of worship. For this reason, many scholars recommend performing **Dhikr** (remembrance of Allah) before beginning the prayer to calm the heart and clear the mind. By focusing on Allah's greatness, mercy, and power, the believer prepares themselves to stand before their Creator with reverence and humility.

Maintaining Khushu in every Salah requires that the individual takes time to understand the meaning of the words they recite. Salah is not just a physical act; it is an intimate conversation with Allah. Every phrase and posture in Salah is filled with profound meaning. By reflecting on these meanings, the worshipper can deepen their connection to the prayer. For example, the phrase **"Subhana Rabbiyal Azeem"** (Glory is to my Lord, the Most Great) uttered during Ruku should remind the believer of the majesty and greatness of Allah. Understanding the words being recited in each part of the prayer helps the heart remain engaged and attentive.

The consistency in Khushu also relies heavily on **Tawheed**—the belief in the oneness of Allah. When a believer fully internalizes the concept of Tawheed, they recognize that their entire existence depends on Allah. This realization fosters a sense of urgency and devotion in their prayers. A person who understands that their sustenance, protection, and guidance come solely from Allah will naturally approach Salah with more humility and concentration. Recognizing Allah's oneness and sovereignty is a powerful way to stay consistent in Khushu because it anchors the mind in the knowledge that no one else can fulfill their needs but Allah.

One way to maintain this awareness is by actively engaging with Allah's names and attributes during prayer. Each name of Allah carries a specific meaning and significance that can guide the believer's focus in Salah. For instance, when reciting **"Alhamdulillahi Rabbil Alameen"** (All praise is due to Allah, the Lord of all that exists) in Surah Al-Fatiha, reflecting on Allah's role as the sustainer of all creation can heighten one's awareness of His majesty. This practice of focusing on Allah's names helps the believer develop a sense of awe and devotion, making it easier to maintain Khushu throughout Salah.

A crucial element in attaining consistency in Khushu is the regularity of Salah itself. Allah has made it obligatory for Muslims to pray five times a day, and these prayers are spread across different parts of the day to ensure that the believer is in constant connection with their Creator. This regularity provides an opportunity for consistent practice, allowing the worshipper to continuously refine their Khushu.

The Prophet Muhammad (peace be upon him) emphasized the importance of maintaining the five daily prayers, as they serve as both a reminder and a spiritual reset throughout the day. He said, **"The first matter that the slave will be brought to account for on the Day of Judgment is the Salah. If it is sound, then the rest of his deeds will be sound. And if it is corrupt, then the rest of his deeds will be corrupt."** This hadith illustrates the centrality of Salah in the life of a Muslim and highlights that the quality of one's prayer, including Khushu, influences the rest of their actions.

The consistency of Salah is also an antidote to the distractions of the world. Each time the believer stands to pray, they are reminded of their ultimate purpose—worshipping Allah. This regular act of submission, when performed with Khushu, fortifies the soul against the temptations and distractions of worldly life. It helps the worshipper recalibrate their intentions and return to a state of mindfulness and devotion.

Consistency in Khushu is further cultivated through a deep understanding of the **etiquettes of Salah**. Every aspect of the prayer, from how one enters the prayer to how one exits, plays a role in establishing focus and humility. The Prophet Muhammad (peace be upon him) was meticulous in his prayers, ensuring that every movement and recitation was done with sincerity and mindfulness. One of the etiquettes that contribute to Khushu is beginning the prayer with **Takbir** (saying Allahu Akbar—Allah is the Greatest) while raising the hands. This act symbolizes leaving behind all worldly concerns and entering into a state of complete submission to Allah.

Another important etiquette is the posture during Salah. The way a person stands, bows, and prostrates reflects their level of Khushu. Standing with the body in an upright position, with hands placed properly and eyes focused on the place of prostration, helps to maintain a sense of stillness and concentration. Similarly, the act of bowing in Ruku and prostrating in Sujood should be done with deliberate calmness, reflecting the submission of the body and soul to Allah.

The physical stillness during Salah also plays a significant role in maintaining consistency in Khushu. The Prophet (peace be upon him) instructed believers to perform each movement in the prayer with tranquility and not to rush through it. He warned against the **hastiness** that many fall into when performing Salah, advising that each posture should be performed with its due right. This means allowing sufficient time for each action to be fully completed, such as staying in Ruku long enough to glorify Allah and remaining in Sujood until a sense of peace is attained.

Another key component to achieving consistent Khushu is through personal reflection. After completing each prayer, it is beneficial to take a moment to reflect on the quality of the Salah. This practice, known as **Muraqabah**, involves assessing one's focus, sincerity, and mindfulness during the prayer.

By regularly evaluating the state of one's Salah, the believer can identify areas of improvement and strive to enhance their Khushu in future prayers.

Muraqabah is not about self-criticism but rather a means of refining the connection with Allah. If the worshipper notices that their mind wandered during prayer, they can make a conscious effort to address the distractions and refocus their heart in the next prayer. The consistent practice of Muraqabah helps the believer develop a deeper awareness of their relationship with Allah, fostering a stronger sense of Khushu over time.

Moreover, the practice of **Istighfar** (seeking forgiveness from Allah) after prayer is another tool to enhance Khushu. By asking for Allah's forgiveness, the believer acknowledges their shortcomings and seeks to purify their soul. The Prophet Muhammad (peace be upon him) used to seek forgiveness after prayer, even though he was free from sin, demonstrating the importance of humility and self-accountability. Istighfar helps to cleanse the heart of any impurities that may have distracted the worshipper during Salah, allowing for a fresh start with each new prayer.

Consistency in Khushu during Salah also requires addressing the root causes of distraction. One of the primary distractions that many people face is the preoccupation with worldly concerns—work, family, financial obligations, and other daily responsibilities. These distractions can take hold of the mind and make it difficult to focus on Allah during prayer. The Prophet Muhammad (peace be upon him) provided guidance on how to manage these distractions, emphasizing the importance of having the correct **Niyyah** (intention) before starting Salah. The act of mentally preparing oneself and making a conscious intention to connect with Allah helps to clear the mind of other concerns, allowing the worshipper to focus on their purpose in the moment.

Another important aspect is ensuring that one's environment is conducive to Khushu. If the place of prayer is cluttered or filled with noise, it becomes much harder to maintain focus. The Prophet (peace be upon him) used to emphasize the importance of simplicity and tranquility in the place of prayer. Praying in a quiet and clean space where distractions are minimized enhances the ability to focus and engage with Allah fully. This also includes avoiding overly ornate clothing or prayer rugs that might attract the gaze away from the prayer itself.

In addition to the physical environment, the **timing of the prayer** also plays a critical role. Allah has set specific times for each prayer, and praying within the early portion of these times is a way to prioritize Salah over other worldly matters. Delaying the prayer unnecessarily often results in a hurried and distracted performance. The Prophet Muhammad (peace be upon him) said, **"The most beloved of deeds to Allah is the prayer performed at its proper time."** Praying on time, with sufficient preparation, ensures that the worshipper can approach Salah without the anxiety of pending tasks or deadlines, fostering a deeper sense of Khushu.

One of the most profound ways to maintain Khushu is through the **remembrance of death**. The Prophet Muhammad (peace be upon him) often encouraged his followers to reflect on the reality of death and the Day of Judgment as a means to strengthen their connection with Allah. The thought of standing before Allah for final accountability can have a powerful impact on how one approaches Salah. When a person prays with the awareness that this prayer could be their last, their sense of urgency and focus naturally increases. This practice serves as a reminder that the ultimate goal of life is to return to Allah, and Salah is the primary means through which one can prepare for that inevitable meeting.

Reflecting on death helps the believer to prioritize their spiritual obligations and detach from the fleeting concerns of the world. It shifts the focus from the temporary to the eternal, making it easier to maintain Khushu during prayer. When the heart is filled with the remembrance of Allah and the Hereafter, worldly distractions lose their significance, and the worshipper becomes more attuned to the presence of Allah during Salah.

In addition to the remembrance of death, it is essential to remember the blessings that Allah has bestowed upon the individual. Reflecting on Allah's countless favors—life, health, family, provision, and guidance—fosters a sense of gratitude and humility. This gratitude, in turn, enhances Khushu, as the worshipper is reminded of their dependence on Allah and their obligation to worship Him sincerely. A grateful heart is naturally more inclined to focus on Allah during Salah, recognizing that every moment of prayer is an opportunity to express thankfulness.

Another method to cultivate consistency in Khushu is by making **Dua (supplication)** for it. The Prophet Muhammad (peace be upon him) taught his companions to ask Allah for help in matters of worship, recognizing that the ability to focus and maintain sincerity in Salah comes from Allah alone. By regularly making Dua for Khushu, the believer acknowledges their need for Allah's guidance and support in perfecting their prayer. One of the Dua's that the Prophet (peace be upon him) used to recite was, **"O Allah, I seek refuge in You from a heart that does not fear (You), and a prayer that is not accepted."** This supplication reminds the worshipper to constantly seek Allah's help in maintaining sincerity and focus in prayer.

Dua also serves as a means of building a closer relationship with Allah. It allows the believer to express their desires, needs, and hopes directly to their Creator. When the believer feels connected to Allah through regular supplication, it becomes easier to maintain Khushu in Salah. This connection nurtures a deep sense of reliance on Allah, reinforcing the understanding that He is the only One who can grant success in both this world and the Hereafter.

Moreover, regular Dua outside of Salah prepares the heart to be more focused during prayer. The act of turning to Allah in moments of need, gratitude, and reflection builds a strong foundation for maintaining Khushu. This is because the believer who constantly engages with Allah in all aspects of life is more likely to remain mindful of Him during Salah.

Consistency in Khushu is also reinforced by adopting a lifestyle that is in harmony with Islamic values and teachings. Engaging in acts of obedience outside of Salah—such as charity, fasting, kindness to others, and staying away from sins—purifies the heart and makes it more receptive to Allah's presence during prayer. The Prophet Muhammad (peace be upon him) said, **"Verily, in the body there is a piece of flesh; if it is sound, the whole body is sound. But if it is corrupt, the whole body is corrupt. Verily, it is the heart."** This hadith illustrates that the state of the heart plays a crucial role in the quality of one's Salah. A heart that is filled with righteousness and obedience will naturally be more inclined to Khushu, while a heart that is tainted with sin and heedlessness will struggle to focus.

One way to purify the heart is by engaging in **Tawbah (repentance)**. Regular repentance for sins, both major and minor, clears the heart of the spiritual diseases that cloud one's focus during Salah. The act of Tawbah softens the heart and makes it more receptive to the remembrance of Allah. When the heart is cleansed through sincere repentance, it becomes easier to maintain Khushu during prayer, as the worshipper is no longer burdened by the weight of sin.

In addition to Tawbah, another method of heart purification is through **giving charity (Sadaqah)**. The Prophet (peace be upon him) emphasized the importance of charity, both as a means of earning Allah's pleasure and as a way to cleanse the heart of attachment to material wealth. When a person gives in charity for the sake of Allah, they are reminded of the transient nature of this world and the eternal rewards of the Hereafter. This detachment from materialism fosters Khushu, as the heart becomes more focused on seeking Allah's pleasure rather than the distractions of the world.

Achieving consistency in Khushu also involves creating healthy habits that support focus and concentration. One such habit is ensuring that the body is well-rested before prayer. Fatigue and exhaustion can significantly hinder one's ability to concentrate during Salah. The Prophet Muhammad (peace be upon him) advised his followers to avoid praying when they are extremely tired or sleepy, as this could affect the quality of their prayer. Ensuring that one is physically rested and mentally alert before beginning Salah enhances the ability to maintain Khushu.

Another habit to develop is proper **time management**. By organizing the day around the five daily prayers, the worshipper places Salah at the center of their schedule, rather than fitting it in around other activities. This prioritization ensures that each prayer is performed without haste or distraction. Managing one's time effectively also prevents the individual from rushing through the prayer in order to attend to other tasks. When Salah is approached with calmness and adequate time, it becomes easier to focus on Allah and maintain Khushu.

In addition to rest and time management, **eating in moderation** is another habit that supports Khushu. Overeating can lead to physical discomfort and drowsiness, making it difficult to focus during Salah. The Prophet Muhammad (peace be upon him) advised his followers to eat in moderation, saying, **"The son of Adam does not fill a container worse than his stomach. It is sufficient for the son of Adam to eat a few mouthfuls to keep him going. But if he must, then a third for food, a third for drink, and a third for air."** By practicing moderation in food intake, the believer can avoid the distractions caused by physical discomfort and maintain a state of focus during Salah.

Another essential habit to develop for maintaining Khushu is **preparing the mind and heart before Salah** through reflection and Dhikr (remembrance of Allah). Before engaging in prayer, one can spend a few minutes reflecting on Allah's greatness, recalling His favors, and reciting words of remembrance like **SubhanAllah (Glory be to Allah), Alhamdulillah (Praise be to Allah), and Allahu Akbar (Allah is the Greatest).** These simple acts of Dhikr help the mind transition from the distractions of daily life to the spiritual focus required in Salah. When the heart is reminded of Allah's majesty and blessings, it becomes easier to approach Salah with humility and a sense of awe, enhancing Khushu.

Dhikr not only prepares the heart for Salah but also serves as a means to cleanse the soul from negative thoughts, worries, and distractions. The more frequently a person engages in Dhikr outside of prayer, the more natural it becomes to maintain focus within prayer. The Prophet Muhammad (peace be upon him) emphasized the importance of keeping the tongue moist with Dhikr, as it purifies the heart and draws the worshipper closer to Allah.

Additionally, reciting short phrases of remembrance after completing each of the five daily prayers helps to extend the state of Khushu beyond the actual prayer itself. This continuous connection to Allah reinforces a mindset of mindfulness and gratitude, making it easier to sustain Khushu in subsequent prayers. Therefore, engaging in regular Dhikr, both before and after Salah, is a powerful tool for nurturing inner tranquility and consistency in Khushu.

Mindfulness of one's posture and physical movements during Salah also plays a significant role in maintaining Khushu. Every movement in Salah has a purpose, from the standing posture in Qiyam to the bowing in Ruku and the prostration in Sujood. The Prophet (peace be upon him) taught that each movement should be performed with deliberation and care, reflecting the seriousness and reverence of standing before Allah. When these actions are rushed or performed carelessly, it undermines the sense of focus and devotion that Khushu requires.

A key aspect of physical mindfulness in Salah is to ensure that each position is completed fully and with stillness before transitioning to the next. This includes ensuring that the body is in a state of calm when standing after Ruku and between the two prostrations. The Prophet (peace be upon him) instructed his companions to avoid moving quickly through Salah as if pecking like a bird, as this diminishes the quality of the prayer. Instead, Salah should be performed with deliberate movements, allowing the worshipper to fully experience each position and the meaning behind it.

Furthermore, the **placement of the gaze** during Salah is essential for maintaining focus. The Prophet Muhammad (peace be upon him) advised worshippers to keep their gaze on the place of prostration during prayer. This simple act helps prevent the mind from wandering and serves as a reminder of the humility and submission required in front of Allah. By keeping the gaze focused and avoiding unnecessary movements or distractions, the worshipper can maintain a state of calm and concentration throughout Salah.

In addition to physical mindfulness, understanding the **meanings and significance of the words recited in Salah** can greatly enhance Khushu. Often, people recite the verses of the Qur'an or the words of remembrance mechanically, without fully grasping their meanings. However, Salah is meant to be a conversation between the worshipper and Allah, and each word carries deep significance. When a person takes the time to understand what they are saying in Salah, their connection to the prayer becomes more profound.

For example, when reciting **Surah Al-Fatiha**, the worshipper is not merely uttering words but is engaging in a dialogue with Allah. The opening chapter of the Qur'an, which is recited in every unit of prayer, contains expressions of praise, supplication, and requests for guidance. By reflecting on the meanings of each verse, the worshipper can develop a stronger sense of Khushu, as they become more aware of their communication with Allah.

Similarly, understanding the significance of **Ruku and Sujood** as acts of humility and submission deepens the emotional experience of Salah. Bowing in Ruku symbolizes the acknowledgment of Allah's greatness, while prostrating in Sujood represents complete submission to His will. When the worshipper internalizes these meanings, each movement in prayer becomes an expression of the heart, enhancing the quality of Khushu and making the prayer more impactful.

Avoiding external distractions is also crucial for maintaining Khushu. In our modern world, distractions are everywhere—whether it's the buzzing of a phone, the noise of people talking, or even the clutter in a room. All of these can pull the mind away from the focus on Allah. Before beginning Salah, it's important to take practical steps to minimize these distractions. This might include turning off phones, finding a quiet space to pray, and ensuring that the surroundings are clean and organized.

The Prophet Muhammad (peace be upon him) taught that the environment in which Salah is performed should be free from distractions, including visual distractions such as patterns on the prayer mat or unnecessary objects in the prayer space. He emphasized that the mind needs clarity and peace in order to connect with Allah. Taking the time to create a serene and distraction-free environment before prayer helps to prevent the mind from being pulled away during Salah, allowing the worshipper to focus fully on their connection with Allah.

In addition to creating a distraction-free environment, it's also important to ensure that the body is comfortable during Salah. Wearing appropriate and comfortable clothing that is suitable for prayer allows the worshipper to move freely without being distracted by discomfort. Furthermore, ensuring that the temperature of the room is comfortable, and that hunger or thirst is not present, contributes to the overall ability to maintain focus during prayer.

Reflecting on the benefits and rewards of Salah can also inspire greater Khushu and devotion. Allah has promised immense rewards for those who perform Salah with sincerity and concentration. The Prophet Muhammad (peace be upon him) said that the first thing a person will be questioned about on the Day of Judgment is their Salah. If the Salah is sound, the rest of their deeds will follow suit, but if the Salah is lacking, the rest of the deeds will be affected. This illustrates the central role that Salah plays in a person's spiritual life and highlights the importance of performing it with Khushu.

Knowing that Salah is a source of immense reward can serve as a powerful motivator to approach it with the reverence it deserves. The Prophet (peace be upon him) also said, **"When a person performs Salah, his sins fall away from him as the leaves fall from the tree."** This powerful imagery illustrates the spiritual purification that takes place during Salah, cleansing the soul and bringing the worshipper closer to Allah.

Reflecting on the **eternal benefits of Salah**, such as closeness to Allah and entry into Paradise, reinforces the importance of maintaining Khushu in prayer. Each prayer is an opportunity to seek Allah's pleasure and forgiveness, and to earn a place in Jannah. By keeping this in mind, the worshipper can approach each Salah with a renewed sense of purpose and dedication, knowing that it is a means to achieve success in this life and the Hereafter.

Another significant aspect of developing Khushu is the **recognition of Salah as a daily retreat from the chaos of life**. In a world that often feels overwhelming, with its constant demands and distractions, Salah offers a unique opportunity to step away from the noise and reconnect with the essence of existence. Each prayer is a personal appointment with Allah, a moment where the heart and soul are allowed to rest and find tranquility in

His presence. Recognizing Salah as a refuge brings a different level of mental and emotional preparedness to prayer, allowing one to approach it with peace and serenity.

The Prophet Muhammad (peace be upon him) is reported to have said, **"The coolness of my eyes is in the prayer."** This statement reflects the deep sense of peace and fulfillment that can be found in Salah when it is performed with Khushu. For the one who truly connects with their Creator during Salah, the world and its concerns fade into the background, and what remains is the serene connection with Allah. In this way, Salah becomes a source of strength, clarity, and comfort, helping the worshipper to face life's challenges with renewed faith and resolve.

This mindset shift—viewing Salah as a retreat rather than an obligation—can dramatically enhance the experience of prayer. Instead of approaching it with a sense of duty or routine, the worshipper looks forward to Salah as a break from the pressures of life, a time to recharge spiritually. When this perspective is internalized, Khushu becomes more natural, as the mind is eager to engage with the peace and tranquility that comes from this sacred moment with Allah.

Developing consistency in Khushu requires an understanding that **spiritual development is gradual**. Often, people feel disheartened when they struggle to maintain Khushu in every prayer, believing that they have failed in their efforts. However, achieving true Khushu is a process that takes time, patience, and persistent effort. Just as physical exercise strengthens the body over time, regular practice and attention to Salah strengthen the soul and its ability to focus in prayer.

It's important to remember that even small improvements in Khushu are valuable and should be celebrated. The Prophet Muhammad (peace be upon him) emphasized the importance of consistency in worship, saying, **"The most beloved deeds to Allah are those done consistently, even if they are small."** This Hadith encourages the believer to maintain steady efforts in improving their Salah, even if the changes seem minor. Over time, these small efforts accumulate, leading to a deeper and more consistent experience of Khushu.

One practical way to track progress is by reflecting on Salah after it is completed. Taking a moment to consider whether there was improvement in focus, concentration, and mindfulness during the prayer allows for self-assessment and goal-setting for the next prayer. By engaging in this reflective practice, worshippers can identify patterns in their behavior, such as particular distractions or moments where the mind wandered, and work to minimize them in future prayers. This methodical approach helps build consistency in Khushu over time.

In order to foster greater **emotional connection during Salah**, it is helpful to personalize the supplications and duas made in prayer. The Prophet Muhammad (peace be upon him) encouraged believers to supplicate to Allah in their own words, expressing their deepest desires, fears, and hopes. While the formal recitations of Salah are prescribed, there is flexibility in the personal supplications made, especially during prostration, which is the moment of greatest closeness to Allah.

The more a worshipper brings their own life and experiences into their supplications, the stronger the emotional connection with Allah becomes. During prostration, a person is in their most humble position, physically and spiritually submitting to Allah's will. This is the ideal time to pour out one's heart in dua, asking for forgiveness, guidance, protection, and all of the needs of this world and the Hereafter. This personal engagement transforms Salah from a ritual into a deeply meaningful conversation with Allah.

Moreover, prostration offers the chance to truly reflect on the worshipper's status as a servant of Allah. It is a physical manifestation of humility, where the forehead touches the ground in acknowledgment of Allah's supremacy and the worshipper's dependence on Him. Understanding this symbolism can invoke a profound sense of humility and gratitude, which in turn enhances Khushu. When a person is aware of their position before their Creator, the heart naturally inclines towards sincerity and focus, deepening the connection during Salah.

Building Khushu also involves recognizing **Salah as a means of seeking Allah's forgiveness**. Each prayer is an opportunity to cleanse the heart and seek pardon for past mistakes. The Prophet Muhammad (peace be upon him) taught that the five daily prayers serve as a form of spiritual purification, washing away sins like a river cleansing a person who bathes in it five times a day. This powerful metaphor illustrates how Salah, when performed with sincerity and concentration, serves to remove the burden of sin and renew the soul.

Reflecting on this aspect of Salah can inspire greater reverence and attentiveness in prayer. Knowing that each prayer is a chance to gain forgiveness from Allah and start afresh can transform the way a person approaches Salah. Instead of viewing it as a routine, the worshipper sees each prayer as a vital moment to seek Allah's mercy and draw closer to Him. This mindset naturally fosters a greater sense of urgency and focus in Salah, leading to a deeper experience of Khushu.

In addition to seeking forgiveness, Salah is also a means of protection from future sins. The Qur'an states, **"Indeed, Salah prevents immorality and wrongdoing"** (Surah Al-Ankabut, 29:45). This verse highlights the role of Salah in cultivating self-discipline and consciousness of Allah, which helps the worshipper avoid sinful behavior. By performing Salah with sincerity and Khushu, a person strengthens their connection to Allah, which in turn acts as a shield against the temptations and misguidances of this world.

Finally, it is important to understand that **Khushu is both an internal and external state**. While the heart plays a central role in developing Khushu, the body must also reflect the reverence and humility required in Salah. The external actions of Salah, such as bowing, prostrating, and standing still, are meant to mirror the internal submission of the heart. When both the heart and body are aligned in worship, the experience of Khushu is complete.

Maintaining this balance requires the worshipper to be conscious of their movements, posture, and gaze throughout the prayer. Each action in Salah should be deliberate and measured, performed with the knowledge that Allah is watching. This physical mindfulness helps prevent the mind from wandering and reinforces the internal focus on Allah. When the body and heart are fully engaged in worship, the prayer becomes a deeply spiritual experience, allowing the worshipper to connect with Allah on a profound level.

As Khushu becomes more consistent, it transforms not only the experience of Salah but also the worshipper's entire relationship with Allah. A person who consistently prays with Khushu develops a stronger sense of humility, gratitude, and reliance on Allah. This connection permeates every aspect of their life, influencing their thoughts, actions, and interactions with others. In this way, Salah serves as both a spiritual anchor and a source of guidance, helping the worshipper navigate the challenges of life with faith and resilience.

13: THE PROPHET'S ﷺ EXAMPLE IN SALAH

The example of the Prophet Muhammad (peace be upon him) in Salah is the most complete and perfect demonstration of how a believer should perform this act of worship. He (PBUH) embodied every element of focus, humility, and reverence that one should strive for in their prayers. His prayers were marked by profound Khushu, which is the deep sense of devotion, humility, and concentration before Allah. Through studying his way of praying, a believer can gain invaluable insights into improving their own Salah and drawing closer to their Creator.

The Prophet's (PBUH) prayer was not just a physical act; it was a heartfelt engagement, reflecting his deep love and connection with Allah. His prayers would often last for hours, especially during the night, as he would stand before his Lord with complete focus. The Prophet's wife, Aisha (may Allah be pleased with her), once asked him, **"Why do you pray until your feet swell when all your sins have been forgiven?"** to which he responded, **"Should I not be a grateful servant?"** This statement encapsulates the essence of his relationship with Allah—prayer was not a duty but a profound expression of gratitude, humility, and servitude.

His example teaches us that Salah should not be seen as a mere obligation but rather as an opportunity to connect with Allah. The outward motions of bowing, prostrating, and standing are to be accompanied by an inward state of surrender, gratitude, and awe. It is in these moments of prayer that a believer truly experiences the closeness to their Creator, as demonstrated by the Messenger of Allah (PBUH).

One of the most remarkable aspects of the Prophet's (PBUH) Salah was his **deep concentration**. The focus he displayed while praying was unshakeable, to the point where even if distractions occurred, they did not deter him from his connection with Allah. It is narrated that once, while praying, the Prophet (PBUH) was presented with a colorful garment, and it slightly distracted him due to its patterns. After finishing the prayer, he immediately instructed that the garment be removed, saying, **"Take this garment away from me, for it distracted me during my prayer."**

This incident highlights the level of mindfulness and attention the Prophet (PBUH) maintained during Salah. His awareness of even the smallest distractions shows how carefully he guarded his heart from anything that could divert his focus away from Allah. For today's believers, this incident serves as a reminder to be mindful of the environment in which they pray and to minimize distractions to maintain Khushu.

In addition to physical distractions, the Prophet (PBUH) was also mindful of **mental distractions**. He would prepare himself for prayer by clearing his mind of worldly concerns and entering into Salah with full attention. He taught his followers that a successful prayer begins with preparation, both mentally and physically. The Prophet (PBUH) would engage in the remembrance of Allah (Dhikr) before beginning his prayer, allowing him to center his heart and mind. This spiritual preparation is an essential part of achieving Khushu and is something that every believer should incorporate into their own prayer routine.

The Prophet's (PBUH) posture and movements during Salah were **slow and deliberate**, reflecting his internal state of Khushu. Each action—whether bowing (Ruku'), prostrating (Sujood), or standing—was performed with precision and calmness. He never rushed through his prayers, even when leading the congregation. This is a significant lesson for those who may find themselves hurrying through Salah, treating it as a task to be completed rather than a moment of connection with Allah.

In one narration, it is reported that a man once prayed hastily in front of the Prophet (PBUH). After the prayer, the Prophet (PBUH) told him, **"Go back and pray, for you have not prayed."** The man, surprised, repeated the prayer in the same hurried manner. After he finished, the Prophet (PBUH) again instructed him to repeat it. This happened several times until the

Prophet (PBUH) finally explained the importance of tranquility and focus in each movement of the prayer. This story serves as a powerful reminder that **Salah is not just about fulfilling the outward form**—it is about the inner state of submission, humility, and stillness before Allah.

By examining the Prophet's (PBUH) example, we see that the quality of each movement in Salah is as important as the quantity. Every bow, prostration, and recitation should be done with care, taking the time to reflect on the meanings of the words being spoken and the significance of the actions being performed.

Another key aspect of the Prophet's (PBUH) Salah was **his emotional connection** to the prayer. He would often be moved to tears during his prayers, especially when reciting verses from the Qur'an that spoke about the Hereafter, Allah's mercy, or His punishment. The Prophet (PBUH) would cry out of love, fear, and awe for his Creator, showing the depth of his sincerity and devotion.

In one instance, Abdullah ibn Shaddad reported that he heard sobbing coming from the chest of the Prophet (PBUH) while he was in Sujood, similar to the sound of boiling water. This demonstrates the profound emotional connection the Prophet (PBUH) had with his Lord during Salah. His prayers were not mechanical or robotic; they were filled with genuine emotion, stemming from his awareness of Allah's majesty and his own dependence on Him.

The Prophet's (PBUH) example reminds believers that **Salah is not merely an intellectual exercise**—it is a deeply personal and emotional experience. When a person truly reflects on the words they are reciting and their position before Allah, they naturally feel a range of emotions, from fear and humility to hope and gratitude. Following the Prophet's (PBUH) model, one should aim to engage both the heart and mind in Salah, allowing the soul to connect with Allah on a deeper level.

The Prophet (PBUH) also taught his followers to be mindful of **the time of Salah**. He would always strive to pray at the earliest possible time for each prayer, demonstrating the importance of prioritizing Salah over other activities. His life revolved around the prayer, and he often reminded his companions of the virtues of praying on time.

It was not uncommon for the Prophet (PBUH) to delay or adjust his other engagements to ensure that he prayed at the most appropriate time. This prioritization of prayer over worldly matters serves as a powerful lesson for modern-day believers, many of whom struggle to balance work, family, and other responsibilities with their prayers. By following the Prophet's (PBUH) example, one can learn to **make prayer the central focus of their daily routine**, allowing it to shape and organize the rest of their life.

In addition, the Prophet (PBUH) emphasized the value of praying in congregation. He would often remind his companions of the rewards associated with congregational prayers and would always encourage them to come to the mosque. The Prophet (PBUH) himself would make every effort to attend the congregational prayers, even when he was sick or tired. His commitment to Salah in congregation highlights the social and communal aspects of prayer, in addition to its personal and spiritual benefits.

One of the most distinctive characteristics of the Prophet's (PBUH) Salah was **his attentiveness to the meanings of the Qur'an**. As he recited the Qur'an during prayer, he would pause at verses that spoke of Allah's mercy or His punishment, reflecting deeply on their meanings. It was not uncommon for the Prophet (PBUH) to weep during these moments, fully absorbing the significance of the divine words.

This practice of reflecting on the meanings of the Qur'an during Salah is an important aspect of achieving Khushu. By paying attention to the words being recited and internalizing their meanings, the worshipper is better able to connect with Allah on a deeper level. The Qur'an is not just a book to be recited—it is a direct communication from Allah to His creation, and understanding its messages is key to fostering a sincere and focused prayer.

The Prophet's (PBUH) habit of **pausing at certain verses** also demonstrates that Salah should not be rushed. There is no need to speed through the recitations or rush from one movement to the next. Instead, Salah should be approached as a calm, reflective practice, where the worshipper takes their time to connect with the words of the Qur'an and the physical actions they are performing. By following this example, one can deepen their connection with Allah and improve the quality of their prayer.

In addition to his focus and emotional connection during Salah, the Prophet (PBUH) emphasized the importance of performing every movement **with**

precision and care. When bowing in Ruku or prostrating in Sujood, the Prophet (PBUH) would make sure that each position was fully established before moving to the next. He once corrected a man who had rushed through his prayer by telling him, **"When you stand to pray, make sure you stand calmly. When you bow, make sure your back is straight and you bow properly. And when you prostrate, make sure you place all of your body parts in their proper positions."**

This teaching is a reminder for believers to focus on the quality of their prayer. The physical actions of Salah are not merely symbolic gestures; they are acts of worship that must be performed with intention and attention. The Prophet's (PBUH) insistence on the correct performance of each movement teaches that **Salah is a comprehensive act**, involving not only the heart and mind but also the body. Each part of the prayer, from standing to bowing, prostrating to sitting, is an opportunity to demonstrate submission and reverence to Allah.

By following the Prophet's (PBUH) example in perfecting the physical aspects of prayer, one also aligns their external actions with their internal state of Khushu. This synchronization between the outward and inward aspects of Salah is essential for achieving the level of devotion that the Prophet (PBUH) exemplified.

The Prophet Muhammad (PBUH) also taught the importance of **remaining consistent in prayer**, regardless of external circumstances. Whether in times of ease or difficulty, the Prophet (PBUH) maintained his commitment to Salah, and this consistency is one of the hallmarks of his devotion. There are numerous instances where the Prophet (PBUH) would pray even when he was tired, sick, or overwhelmed with responsibilities. His actions reflect a deep understanding of the role of prayer in sustaining a believer through life's challenges.

For believers today, this consistency in prayer serves as a powerful example. In modern life, there are countless distractions and responsibilities that can pull a person away from their spiritual duties. However, by following the Prophet's (PBUH) example, one can learn to prioritize prayer, even in the busiest or most difficult of times. **Salah becomes a source of strength—**a means of finding solace and stability amidst the trials of life.

The Prophet's (PBUH) practice of praying during the night (Tahajjud) is another profound example of his consistency. Even after a long day, he would still find time to wake up in the quiet hours of the night to stand in prayer. This reflects his understanding that **Salah is not merely a ritual**—it is a vital connection between the believer and Allah, a connection that must be nurtured through consistency and dedication.

The **length of the Prophet's (PBUH) prayers** also varied depending on the circumstances. When praying alone or during the night prayers (Qiyam ul-Layl), the Prophet (PBUH) would often prolong his prayers, standing for long periods of time reciting the Qur'an, bowing deeply, and remaining in prostration for extended periods. This practice demonstrated his love for spending time in prayer and his desire to be in the presence of Allah for as long as possible.

However, when leading the congregation, the Prophet (PBUH) would shorten his prayers, making them easy for the people behind him. He understood that not everyone could pray for as long as he could, and he took into consideration the needs of the elderly, the sick, and those with other responsibilities. This balance between lengthening and shortening the prayers according to the situation reflects the Prophet's (PBUH) wisdom and consideration for others.

For believers today, this example teaches the importance of **adapting one's prayer** according to the circumstances. When praying alone, one can take their time and immerse themselves in worship. However, when praying with others, particularly in congregational prayers, it is important to be mindful of the needs of those around you. By following the Prophet's (PBUH) example, one can learn to be both a devoted worshipper and a compassionate leader.

The **physical preparation for Salah** is another crucial aspect of the Prophet's (PBUH) example. He would always ensure that he was in a state of physical cleanliness before praying, as this is a key requirement for the acceptance of Salah. Wudu (ablution) was performed with great care and attention, as the Prophet (PBUH) taught that cleanliness is half of faith. His Wudu was done meticulously, ensuring that every part required for washing was thoroughly cleansed.

In addition to performing Wudu, the Prophet (PBUH) would wear clean clothes and use perfume (if available) before prayer, reflecting his deep respect for the act of worship he was about to engage in. This level of preparation demonstrates that Salah is not an ordinary act—it is a meeting with the Creator and should be approached with the utmost care and reverence.

The Prophet's (PBUH) emphasis on physical cleanliness before Salah also reflects a broader principle in Islam: that **spiritual cleanliness** is closely linked to physical cleanliness. Just as one purifies their body before standing in prayer, they should also strive to purify their heart and mind. This means entering into Salah with sincere intention, free from worldly distractions, and focusing solely on worshipping Allah.

The **Prophet's (PBUH) interaction with his companions during Salah** also offers valuable lessons. While leading the prayers, the Prophet (PBUH) was acutely aware of the needs of those behind him. If he heard a child crying, for instance, he would shorten the prayer out of compassion for the mother. This act of kindness and understanding reflects the Prophet's (PBUH) deep empathy and his desire to ease the burdens of those around him.

By shortening the prayer in such circumstances, the Prophet (PBUH) demonstrated that **compassion and consideration** should always be present in worship. Salah is a means of connecting with Allah, but it should never be a burden on others. This lesson is especially relevant for those who lead congregational prayers, reminding them to be mindful of the needs of their community and to approach leadership with empathy and care.

For modern believers, this teaches the importance of being aware of others' circumstances, even in acts of worship. Whether leading the prayer or participating in a group, one should always strive to create an environment of ease, comfort, and compassion. The Prophet's (PBUH) ability to balance his own devotion with the needs of his companions exemplifies his unmatched wisdom and understanding.

The **Prophet's (PBUH) prayers for the Ummah** during his Salah were a reflection of his boundless love and concern for his followers. It is reported that during his night prayers, he would frequently pray for the forgiveness and well-being of his Ummah, showing his deep care for their spiritual success. Even during his final days, when he was suffering from illness, the Prophet (PBUH) continued to pray for his people, seeking Allah's mercy and guidance for them.

This intercessory aspect of the Prophet's (PBUH) prayer is a reminder for every believer to **pray not only for themselves but also for others**. In Salah, one has the opportunity to ask Allah for blessings, mercy, and forgiveness, not only for themselves but for their family, friends, and the wider Ummah. This communal aspect of prayer reflects the interconnectedness of the Muslim community and the importance of caring for one another's spiritual well-being.

By following the Prophet's (PBUH) example, believers can cultivate a deeper sense of empathy and care for others in their prayers. This habit of praying for the community, for the suffering, and for those in need helps to reinforce the bonds of brotherhood and sisterhood in Islam, fostering a stronger and more compassionate Ummah.

The Prophet (PBUH) was also careful to **avoid excessive movements during prayer**, ensuring that his attention was solely on Allah. He maintained a stillness that reflected his inner state of submission and concentration. Any unnecessary movement was avoided, and his body was calm and composed throughout the prayer. This physical stillness is a manifestation of Khushu, as it helps the worshipper maintain focus and avoid distractions.

For believers today, this serves as a reminder to minimize distractions during Salah. Whether it's fidgeting, looking around, or allowing one's mind to wander, these actions can detract from the quality of the prayer. The Prophet's (PBUH) example teaches that **Salah should be approached with a sense of stillness and reverence**, allowing the heart and mind to focus entirely on Allah. By reducing unnecessary movements, a person can achieve a deeper sense of peace and concentration in their prayers.

Moreover, the Prophet (PBUH) taught his companions to maintain this stillness and focus even when facing external distractions. In one instance, a companion was seen playing with his beard during Salah, and the Prophet (PBUH) remarked that if his heart had been focused, his body would have been too. This profound statement reflects the deep connection between the heart and the body in Salah—when the heart is engaged, the body naturally follows in submission.

The Prophet (PBUH) also taught that **Salah is a means of seeking Allah's protection and guidance**. In times of difficulty or distress, the Prophet (PBUH) would turn to Salah, seeking comfort and solutions from Allah.

When faced with challenges, whether personal or communal, he would rise in prayer, asking Allah for guidance and strength. This habit of turning to Salah in times of need highlights the central role that prayer plays in the life of a believer.

For modern believers, the Prophet's (PBUH) example teaches that **Salah is not just a routine**—it is a powerful tool for navigating life's difficulties. When faced with uncertainty, anxiety, or hardship, Salah provides a way to seek Allah's help and to find solace in His presence. By following the Prophet's (PBUH) example, one can learn to rely on prayer not only as an obligation but as a source of strength, comfort, and guidance.

The Prophet (PBUH) demonstrated this practice during significant events in his life. Whether preparing for battle, making important decisions, or seeking Allah's forgiveness, the Prophet (PBUH) always began with prayer. This reliance on Allah through Salah is a powerful lesson for all believers, reminding them that **prayer is the ultimate refuge** in both times of ease and difficulty.

In addition to his reliance on Salah during times of hardship, the Prophet (PBUH) exemplified the power of prayer as a means of cultivating **gratitude and humility**. Every moment spent in prayer was an expression of gratitude to Allah for the countless blessings bestowed upon him and the Ummah. The Prophet (PBUH) often encouraged his companions to remember that everything they had, whether material or spiritual, was from Allah and that prayer was a means of showing thanks.

The Prophet (PBUH) would regularly pray late into the night, and when Aisha (RA) asked him why he prayed so much even though his past and future sins were forgiven, he replied, **"Should I not be a grateful servant?"** This statement captures the essence of the Prophet's (PBUH) relationship with Allah—one of profound gratitude. Despite his high status and closeness to Allah, the Prophet (PBUH) never ceased to humble himself in prayer, recognizing that all power, all sustenance, and all blessings come from the Creator alone.

For modern believers, this lesson in gratitude is transformative. In a world filled with distractions and material pursuits, Salah serves as a reminder to pause and reflect on the blessings in one's life. By following the Prophet's (PBUH) example, believers can cultivate a deep sense of humility, recognizing that every breath, every heartbeat, and every moment of their existence is a gift from Allah.

The **Prophet's (PBUH) care for his companions and the wider community** was also reflected in how he approached congregational prayers. He placed great emphasis on the unity of the Ummah, and Salah was one of the most significant acts that brought people together. In his leadership, the Prophet (PBUH) encouraged believers to pray in congregation as much as possible, stating that the reward for praying in congregation was 27 times greater than praying alone.

The Prophet's (PBUH) insistence on congregational prayers underscores the importance of community in Islam. Salah is not just a personal act of devotion; it is a collective one that fosters a sense of brotherhood and sisterhood among believers. By praying together, the Ummah becomes more united, and this unity strengthens the fabric of the Muslim community.

Furthermore, the Prophet (PBUH) would always make sure that everyone felt included and cared for in the congregational prayers. He would check on his companions, ensuring that no one was left behind or felt alienated. This deep sense of compassion and care highlights the communal nature of Salah, encouraging believers to not only focus on their own prayers but also be mindful of those around them. **The unity of the believers in Salah reflects the unity of the Ummah**—a bond that transcends differences and brings people together in worship.

The Prophet (PBUH) also taught that **Salah is a shield against sins and immoral behavior**. In one of his sayings, the Prophet (PBUH) mentioned that prayer serves as a means of cleansing the believer from their mistakes and transgressions. He explained to his companions that just as a person who bathes in a river five times a day would emerge clean, so too does the believer who prays five times daily emerge spiritually cleansed.

This analogy of prayer as a form of purification highlights its transformative power. Each Salah provides the believer with an opportunity to seek forgiveness and renew their commitment to Allah. By turning to Allah throughout the day in prayer, a person becomes more conscious of their actions, thoughts, and words. The connection to Allah is continually strengthened, and this connection helps the believer avoid behaviors that are displeasing to Allah.

For modern believers, this aspect of Salah as a form of spiritual purification is essential. In a world where temptations and distractions are abundant, prayer serves as a **means of protecting one's heart and mind**. By consistently turning to Allah in Salah, one becomes more aware of their actions and more focused on living a life that is pleasing to Allah. The Prophet's (PBUH) example reminds believers that Salah is not just an obligation—it is a tool for moral and spiritual growth.

One of the most profound lessons that the Prophet (PBUH) imparted regarding Salah is that **prayer should be approached with sincerity and focus**. The Prophet (PBUH) taught that **the quality of one's prayer is more important than the quantity**. He emphasized the importance of praying with a sincere heart, focusing entirely on Allah, and avoiding distractions. The Prophet (PBUH) once said, **"A person may finish their prayer and receive no reward except for one-tenth of it, one-ninth, one-eighth, one-seventh, one-sixth, one-fifth, one-fourth, one-third, or half of it."** This statement highlights that the reward for Salah is directly related to the amount of focus and devotion one puts into it.

The Prophet (PBUH) would frequently remind his companions to pray as if they were seeing Allah, for even though they could not see Allah, they should be conscious that Allah was always watching them. This level of awareness— known as **Ihsan**—is the highest level of faith, where a person prays with full consciousness of Allah's presence.

For believers, this teaching serves as a powerful reminder to approach Salah with sincerity and humility. It's not enough to go through the motions of prayer; one must engage their heart and mind in the act of worship. **True Salah requires focus, sincerity, and a deep sense of connection to Allah**, qualities that the Prophet (PBUH) embodied in every prayer he offered.

The Prophet (PBUH) also taught that Salah should not be rushed. He emphasized the importance of **taking one's time during prayer**, making sure that each position is fully established before moving on to the next. Rushing through Salah diminishes its quality and the sense of connection to Allah. The Prophet (PBUH) warned against this by saying, **"The worst thief is the one who steals from his prayer."** When asked how someone could steal from their prayer, he replied, **"By not performing the bowing and prostration properly."**

This teaching highlights that Salah is not just about the words or the outward movements—it's about the **inner state of the worshipper**. Rushing through prayer can cause a person to lose focus and diminish the quality of their worship. The Prophet (PBUH) showed that each movement in Salah is an opportunity to reflect, to be still, and to connect with Allah on a deeper level.

By following the Prophet's (PBUH) example, believers can learn to slow down during Salah, giving each part of the prayer its due attention. This approach not only improves the quality of the prayer but also strengthens one's connection to Allah. **Salah is a time for reflection, peace, and connection**, and rushing through it robs the believer of these benefits.

Finally, the Prophet (PBUH) also taught the importance of **making dua (supplication) within Salah**. After completing the obligatory parts of the prayer, the Prophet (PBUH) would often make dua, asking Allah for guidance, forgiveness, and mercy. He encouraged his companions to do the same, teaching them that the moments during and after Salah are powerful times for supplication.

This practice of making dua in Salah reflects the **intimate nature of the relationship between the believer and Allah**. Salah is not just a ritual—it is a conversation with Allah, a time to pour out one's heart, seek Allah's help, and express gratitude. The Prophet (PBUH) showed that after completing the obligatory acts of worship, one should take advantage of the time to make personal supplications, asking Allah for whatever they need.

For modern believers, this practice serves as a reminder that **Salah is a time of connection and communication with Allah**. After completing the prayer, one should take a moment to engage in heartfelt dua, asking Allah for guidance, strength, and protection. This habit of making dua after Salah helps to reinforce the personal connection between the believer and their Creator, making prayer not just an obligation but a deeply personal act of worship.

14: THE CONNECTION BETWEEN TAWHEED AND KHUSHU

At the core of **Khushu in Salah** lies the recognition of **Tawheed**, the oneness of Allah. This principle forms the foundation of all acts of worship in Islam, including Salah. Tawheed is not merely an intellectual understanding; it is the essence that transforms one's approach to worship. It is through this deep-rooted belief in the oneness of Allah that a Muslim finds the humility, sincerity, and focus necessary for a prayer filled with Khushu.

The Qur'an frequently calls believers to reflect on the oneness of Allah, reinforcing the idea that there is no deity worthy of worship except Him. In Surah Al-Baqarah, Allah says, **"And your god is One God. There is no deity [worthy of worship] except Him, the Most Merciful, the Especially Merciful."** (Qur'an 2:163). This verse, along with many others, guides the believer to internalize the idea that only Allah holds ultimate authority over all matters in life and death.

When this recognition of Allah's oneness permeates the heart, it impacts not just the outward aspects of prayer, but also the inner state of the worshiper. Salah becomes a moment of intimate connection with the Creator, a time to remind oneself that all power, all authority, and all mercy belong to Allah alone. **Tawheed is the lens through which Khushu is achieved—** without it, Salah loses its meaning and purpose.

The relationship between **Tawheed and Khushu** becomes clearer when we understand that **Tawheed instills humility and dependence** on Allah. When a believer approaches Salah with the firm belief that there is no god but Allah, they stand in a state of complete submission. There is no need for pride or arrogance, for everything one possesses is from Allah, and only He has the power to give and take.

The **first part of the Shahada**, "La ilaha illallah" (There is no god but

Allah), shapes the very essence of Khushu. It reminds the believer that every action, including Salah, should be directed toward seeking the pleasure of Allah alone. This sense of purpose leads to **a deep sense of awe** and reverence during prayer, which is the foundation of Khushu.

A person who understands Tawheed is conscious of the fact that Allah is the only One who can hear their prayers, see their sincerity, and judge their actions. This consciousness naturally leads to greater focus, humility, and attentiveness in Salah. The distractions of the world fade away, and the heart is filled with **the sole desire to connect with Allah**.

It is also important to remember that **Tawheed entails recognizing Allah as the only source of guidance and help**. Allah says in the Qur'an, **"It is You we worship and You we ask for help"** (Qur'an 1:5). This verse, recited in every unit of prayer, reinforces the believer's reliance on Allah alone for success, guidance, and support in all affairs.

A believer who embodies Tawheed approaches Salah with the knowledge that **only Allah can grant them peace, forgiveness, and mercy**. This awareness drives the worshipper to seek Khushu, as they recognize the weight of their prayer and the power of the One they are standing before. **The realization of Allah's greatness humbles the heart**, allowing it to focus solely on the act of worship and block out any distractions.

Understanding that **Allah controls all affairs** helps believers surrender completely in Salah, focusing on their spiritual connection rather than being consumed by their daily worries. The more a person strengthens their understanding of Tawheed, the more profound their Khushu becomes, because they no longer rely on anything or anyone else but Allah.

The concept of **Tawheed also influences the way believers view their relationship with the world**. When a Muslim fully grasps that Allah is the sole Creator and Sustainer of the universe, they stop giving undue importance to material possessions, status, or worldly achievements. In Salah, this translates into greater **focus and mindfulness**, as the distractions of the dunya (world) become insignificant in comparison to the magnificence of Allah.

When a believer prays with a heart filled with Tawheed, they realize that **nothing in this world can bring them true success** except their relationship with Allah. This understanding compels them to approach Salah with sincerity, knowing that **Allah alone has control over their destiny**. Such a person prays not to seek validation from others, but solely to earn the pleasure of Allah, thereby deepening their Khushu.

Furthermore, the belief in **Tawheed Rububiyyah** (the oneness of Allah's lordship) ensures that the worshiper is aware of Allah's constant presence and supervision. **Allah is always watching**, and this knowledge strengthens the believer's determination to pray with Khushu, as they are conscious of Allah's all-encompassing awareness. Every bow, every prostration, and every word in Salah becomes a sincere act of worship, directed towards the One who knows the innermost thoughts of the heart.

A key aspect of Tawheed is the concept of **Tawheed Al-Uluhiyyah**, which refers to the oneness of Allah in His worship. This form of Tawheed teaches that only Allah deserves to be worshiped and that no act of worship should be directed toward anyone or anything other than Him. This concept is crucial in developing Khushu because it reminds the believer that **Salah is an exclusive and intimate interaction between the servant and their Creator**.

When a person recognizes the significance of **worshiping Allah alone**, they are compelled to approach their prayer with a deep sense of devotion. They are aware that this time is sacred and that **no one else is worthy of their attention or devotion** during Salah. Tawheed Al-Uluhiyyah thus elevates the act of prayer to a higher plane of spiritual consciousness, where the heart is fully engaged in worship and connected solely to Allah.

This form of Tawheed also prevents any form of **showing off or seeking the praise of others** in prayer, as the believer knows that only Allah's approval matters. The Prophet (PBUH) warned against the dangers of performing acts of worship for the sake of others, calling it a form of hidden shirk. A person who understands Tawheed avoids such pitfalls and strives to ensure that their Salah is performed with sincerity, humility, and Khushu.

Tawheed also provides protection against shirk (associating partners with Allah), which can manifest in both major and subtle forms. Even minor forms of shirk, such as seeking approval from others or performing acts of worship for show, can diminish the effectiveness of Salah and weaken one's Khushu. When a person holds firm to the principles of Tawheed, they guard their Salah from being contaminated by such impurities.

The Qur'an emphasizes the importance of worshiping Allah alone and warns against the dangers of shirk. Allah says, **"Indeed, Allah does not forgive association with Him, but He forgives what is less than that for whom He wills"** (Qur'an 4:48). This verse serves as a stern reminder of the gravity of shirk and the importance of preserving the purity of one's worship.

By adhering to Tawheed, believers protect their **spiritual connection with Allah** and ensure that their prayers are filled with sincerity. The purity of their intention, grounded in Tawheed, allows them to experience a heightened sense of Khushu. Every moment in prayer becomes an opportunity to renew their commitment to Allah and strengthen their reliance on Him alone.

When a believer contemplates the significance of **Tawheed Al-Asma wa Sifat**—the oneness of Allah's names and attributes—it enhances their understanding of who Allah is, and this deepens their sense of awe and reverence in prayer. Allah's names, such as **Al-'Aleem** (the All-Knowing), **Ar-Rahman** (the Most Merciful), and **Al-Malik** (the King), reflect His absolute perfection and control over all matters.

Incorporating this understanding into Salah, a believer recognizes that they are standing before **the One who knows everything about them**, their innermost thoughts, and their deepest desires. This realization brings a powerful sense of humility and sincerity, which forms the core of Khushu. When a person reflects on Allah's attributes, such as His mercy, knowledge, and power, it leads to greater mindfulness and focus in Salah.

Each attribute of Allah serves as a reminder of His greatness and our dependence on Him. The believer, through Tawheed Al-Asma wa Sifat, acknowledges that **only Allah possesses the perfect qualities** necessary to respond to their prayers. This conviction leads the worshiper to surrender fully, concentrating on the fact that they are invoking the One whose power is unmatched and whose mercy is boundless. This awareness fuels their Khushu, driving them to pray with complete attentiveness and devotion.

An essential part of Khushu is to consistently remind oneself of Allah's **omnipresence and omnipotence**. Through Tawheed, the worshiper understands that Allah is not only the Creator but also the Sustainer of all things. In Surah Al-Ikhlas, Allah declares, **"Say, 'He is Allah, [Who is] One, Allah, the Eternal Refuge.'"** (Qur'an 112:1-2). This short yet powerful chapter underscores the centrality of Tawheed in the life of a believer, reminding them that all things return to Allah, the Self-Sufficient and Everlasting.

In moments of Salah, when one fully reflects on the perfection of Allah's attributes, they naturally adopt a posture of humility. Khushu becomes the outcome of acknowledging that **Allah controls all matters**, and that every breath, every thought, and every movement is within His knowledge and power. A person praying with this awareness lets go of the distractions of the dunya and allows themselves to be fully present in front of Allah, recognizing that no one else holds any control over their fate.

Moreover, the awareness of **Allah's mercy** invites a deep sense of gratitude. A heart filled with gratitude is one that bows low in Khushu. The worshiper understands that even their ability to stand in prayer is a gift from Allah, a sign of His boundless mercy. This recognition of Allah's continuous favors inspires a profound connection during Salah, one in which Khushu flourishes.

As believers grow in their understanding of **Tawheed**, they begin to see how it influences their perspective on the dunya. The realization that **Allah alone provides for their needs** reduces their attachment to worldly affairs, allowing them to focus more on their spiritual responsibilities. In prayer, this translates to a more focused, calm, and sincere act of worship, as the believer's heart becomes less distracted by material concerns and more anchored in their relationship with Allah.

This detachment from the dunya is critical in achieving Khushu. A person who understands that **wealth, status, and success** come solely from Allah no longer spends their Salah thinking about worldly pursuits. Instead, they turn their full attention to Allah, knowing that **true success lies in pleasing Him**. Tawheed helps the believer to strike a balance between fulfilling worldly obligations and maintaining a firm connection with Allah, ensuring that their Salah is not compromised by thoughts of worldly gain or loss.

Furthermore, the believer who understands Tawheed also recognizes that every trial and blessing comes from Allah. This realization encourages them to approach Salah with a heart full of trust in Allah's plan. They turn to Allah in moments of hardship, fully aware that only He can ease their burden. This reliance on Allah alone cultivates Khushu, as the believer prays with a sense of total surrender and hope.

Through the lens of Tawheed, the **duas made in Salah take on new significance**. When a worshiper calls upon Allah, fully realizing His attributes of mercy, power, and wisdom, they are filled with confidence that their prayers are being heard. This certainty that Allah is listening brings the worshiper closer to Khushu, as they pour their heart into their supplications, knowing that no effort is wasted when seeking help from Allah.

Tawakkul (trust in Allah) is a natural extension of Tawheed. When a believer trusts that Allah alone is in control, they develop a sense of tranquility during prayer. The anxiety and restlessness that often plague the heart during difficult times are replaced with calmness and reliance on Allah. This inner peace is a crucial element of Khushu, as it allows the believer to focus on the act of worship rather than being consumed by worry or fear.

This sense of **total reliance on Allah** also leads to an increase in sincerity. When a person prays with the knowledge that **only Allah has the power to answer their duas**, their intention is purified. The desire to impress others or gain worldly benefits from prayer fades away, and what remains is a pure, sincere act of worship. **Sincerity** is one of the most important aspects of Khushu, as it directs the heart solely toward Allah.

One of the key fruits of Tawheed is the **profound sense of accountability** it instills in the believer. Tawheed teaches that every person will stand alone before Allah on the Day of Judgment and be accountable for their deeds. This awareness brings a heightened sense of seriousness to Salah, as the worshiper recognizes that their prayer is a means of preparing for the ultimate reckoning.

When a person prays with the understanding that **Allah is both the Judge and the Merciful**, their Khushu deepens. They know that their prayer is not just a routine task but a precious opportunity to seek forgiveness, express gratitude, and ask for guidance. The believer's heart trembles with awe at the thought of standing before Allah, the Judge, and this trembling leads to Khushu. The fear of accountability, coupled with hope in Allah's mercy, creates a balanced approach to worship, where the believer prays with both reverence and love.

Furthermore, the **belief in the Hereafter**, which is deeply tied to Tawheed, motivates the worshiper to make their Salah meaningful. The thought that **this life is temporary and the Hereafter is eternal** encourages the believer to invest time and effort into perfecting their Salah. They are not content with simply going through the motions, but they strive to offer Salah that is filled with devotion and Khushu, knowing that it will weigh heavily in the scales of justice on the Day of Judgment.

The more a person grows in their understanding of Tawheed, the more they realize that Salah is a means of drawing closer to Allah. It is through Salah that the believer can connect with their Creator, seek His help, and ask for guidance. This realization brings about a **sense of longing** in the heart—a desire to be near Allah, to be enveloped in His mercy, and to gain His pleasure.

This longing leads to **greater focus and concentration** in Salah. The worshiper approaches prayer with a heart that yearns for Allah, and this yearning translates into Khushu. They are no longer distracted by worldly concerns, because their heart is fully occupied with thoughts of Allah. This level of devotion can only be achieved through a deep understanding of Tawheed, as it reminds the believer that **Allah is the ultimate source of peace, contentment, and success.**

A believer who contemplates the reality of Tawheed begins to understand that **Allah's presence permeates every aspect of their life**, not just the moments in prayer. This realization transforms the way they approach their entire day, making them more mindful of their actions and their state of heart even outside of Salah. The deeper the awareness of Tawheed, the more consistent they become in maintaining Khushu, not just within the confines of prayer, but as a lasting state of humility, gratitude, and mindfulness of Allah.

This broader application of Khushu, extending beyond the prayer mat, means that the believer carries the consciousness of Allah's greatness throughout their daily life. **Every action, every decision, every word spoken** is imbued with the awareness that Allah is watching, hearing, and knowing everything. This helps the believer avoid arrogance, heedlessness, or selfish behavior, which are major obstacles to Khushu.

By living with the understanding that Allah alone is worthy of worship and submission, the believer is constantly reminded of their reliance on Allah. This reliance not only fosters humility but also shields the believer from falling into the trap of pride or self-sufficiency, further deepening the state of Khushu. **Tawheed reinforces the believer's consciousness** that nothing happens without the will of Allah, which in turn strengthens their sense of reverence in all acts of worship.

The concept of **complete submission to Allah**—a fundamental tenet of Tawheed—is closely tied to Khushu. True submission means that the believer recognizes they have no power or control except by the permission of Allah. This acknowledgment strips away any sense of self-importance or entitlement, which are barriers to experiencing Khushu.

When standing in prayer, the believer feels **humbled and small before the majesty of Allah**. They are reminded that their life, their success, and even their ability to pray is a gift from Allah. This sense of dependency fosters a deeper level of sincerity and attentiveness in Salah, as the believer stands with the full realization that they are in need of Allah's mercy, guidance, and forgiveness.

Furthermore, the realization of Allah's supreme authority and power compels the believer to strive for excellence in worship. **Tawheed drives the worshiper to offer their best** in Salah, knowing that they are standing before the One who controls everything in the heavens and the earth. This striving for excellence naturally leads to Khushu, as the believer is motivated to focus fully on their prayer, ensuring that it is performed with the utmost care and devotion.

The journey toward achieving Khushu is deeply intertwined with the journey of perfecting one's understanding and practice of Tawheed. As the believer progresses in their knowledge of Allah's oneness, they become more aware of the distractions and weaknesses that pull them away from Khushu. Through Tawheed, they learn to overcome these distractions by grounding themselves in the reality that **Allah is always near, always watching, and always in control**.

One of the most common obstacles to Khushu is the wandering mind, which often drifts toward thoughts of worldly concerns during Salah. The teachings of Tawheed remind the believer that **these concerns are fleeting and temporary**, whereas their connection with Allah is eternal and far more significant. By focusing on the hereafter and trusting in Allah's plan, the believer can push aside these distractions and concentrate fully on their prayer.

Tawheed also helps the believer recognize the **true purpose of life**: to worship Allah and seek His pleasure. This realization shifts the focus away from trivial matters and redirects the heart toward fulfilling the higher purpose of existence. The more a believer internalizes this purpose, the more naturally Khushu develops, as the distractions of the dunya lose their grip on the heart.

Tawheed strengthens the believer's resolve to constantly seek forgiveness and turn to Allah with humility. Knowing that Allah is **Al-Ghaffar** (The Forgiving) and **At-Tawwab** (The Accepter of Repentance), the believer is motivated to approach Salah not just as a ritual, but as an opportunity to cleanse the soul and draw nearer to Allah.

This understanding transforms Salah into a deeply personal and reflective act of worship. **Each time the believer prays**, they are reminded of Allah's endless mercy and forgiveness, which softens the heart and fosters Khushu. The act of seeking forgiveness during Salah becomes a moment of sincere reflection on one's shortcomings and a reminder of Allah's overwhelming generosity in accepting repentance.

Moreover, Tawheed reinforces the concept that **Allah alone forgives sins**. This knowledge brings a sense of urgency to Salah, as the believer realizes that no other means can cleanse the soul or bring about Allah's mercy except through sincere worship and repentance. This realization heightens the importance of Salah in the believer's life, driving them to approach it with renewed focus and humility.

As the believer's understanding of Tawheed deepens, so does their sense of **gratitude** for Allah's countless blessings. Every aspect of life, from the air they breathe to the ability to perform Salah, is a reminder of Allah's mercy and generosity. This profound sense of gratitude fuels Khushu, as the believer stands in prayer, overwhelmed by the realization that **everything they have is a gift from Allah**.

Gratitude transforms the way a person prays. Instead of approaching Salah as a mere obligation, the believer sees it as a chance to express their appreciation for Allah's favors. **Khushu becomes a natural response** to this feeling of gratitude, as the heart is filled with love and reverence for the One who has given them more than they could ever repay.

In addition to fostering Khushu, gratitude also helps the believer maintain a positive and hopeful mindset, even in times of difficulty. Through Tawheed, the believer understands that even challenges and hardships are a part of Allah's divine plan and that they carry wisdom and mercy. This realization enables the believer to approach Salah with a heart that is both humble and content, further deepening their state of Khushu.

Tawheed also teaches the believer the importance of **maintaining a balance between fear and hope** in their relationship with Allah. While fear of Allah's justice and accountability fosters humility and reverence, hope in His mercy and forgiveness encourages the believer to strive for improvement and closeness to Allah. This balance is critical in achieving Khushu, as it prevents the believer from falling into despair or complacency.

In Salah, this balance is reflected in the way the believer approaches each act of worship. They pray with **the fear of falling short in their duties** and the hope that Allah will accept their efforts, no matter how small. This dual approach ensures that the heart remains engaged and sincere, which are essential components of Khushu.

Moreover, **Tawheed Al-Rububiyyah**—the belief that Allah is the Sustainer and Provider of all things—reinforces this balance. The believer understands that Allah is both the Creator and the Judge, and that He rewards those who turn to Him in sincerity. This knowledge strengthens the believer's resolve to perform Salah with full attention and devotion, knowing that Allah's mercy and justice are perfectly balanced.

The teachings of Tawheed guide the believer toward **constant self-reflection and self-improvement**. By recognizing that their ultimate purpose is to worship Allah alone, the believer is driven to assess their actions, intentions, and level of sincerity. This introspection naturally leads to Khushu, as the believer strives to ensure that their Salah is a true reflection of their submission to Allah.

One of the most powerful aspects of Tawheed is that it removes the believer's dependence on anyone or anything other than Allah. **This sense of independence** from the material world frees the believer's heart from distractions and worries, allowing them to focus solely on their relationship with Allah during Salah. With no other concerns pulling them away, the believer can fully immerse themselves in the act of worship, experiencing Khushu in its purest form.

In this way, Tawheed acts as a shield against the common distractions that often plague the mind during Salah. By reminding the believer of Allah's oneness and control over all things, it grounds their thoughts and helps them maintain a focused and sincere connection with their Creator.

Tawheed also teaches the believer to **value the time spent in worship**. Understanding that every moment in Salah is an opportunity to connect with Allah and seek His mercy, the believer approaches prayer with a sense of urgency and importance. This heightened awareness of the value of worship naturally leads to Khushu, as the believer strives to make the most of each moment in Salah.

Moreover, Tawheed instills a sense of **accountability and responsibility** in the believer. Knowing that they will one day stand before Allah and be questioned about their deeds, including their Salah, the believer is motivated to perform each prayer with care and devotion. This sense of accountability fosters Khushu, as the believer seeks to offer their best in every act of worship, knowing that it will be weighed on the Day of Judgment.

Through Tawheed, the believer learns that **Salah is more than just a ritual**—it is a profound act of worship that brings them closer to Allah and strengthens their relationship with Him. This understanding transforms the way the believer approaches prayer, ensuring that each Salah is filled with sincerity, humility, and Khushu.

15: SALAH AND THE AFTERLIFE

The connection between **Salah and the afterlife** is profound and undeniable. In the Qur'an, Allah repeatedly reminds us that our success in the Hereafter is directly linked to our worship in this world. Among the foremost acts of worship, **Salah stands as the pillar of Islam**, and its impact on our eternal destination cannot be overstated. Salah is not merely an obligation or a routine, but a profound connection with our Creator. It is the pathway to His mercy, a shield against sin, and the means by which the believer's soul is nurtured and prepared for the ultimate reality of the Hereafter.

The **Day of Judgment** will be a day of immense accountability. Every deed, small or large, will be weighed. In this context, the Prophet Muhammad (PBUH) taught us that the first matter to be examined from a servant's deeds will be their Salah. If the Salah is found to be in order, then the rest of the deeds will follow suit. This shows the centrality of Salah to one's success in the Hereafter. The believer is made to understand that Salah is not just a fleeting act, but the foundation of their success in the life to come.

It is essential to view Salah as **a divine investment**. Every prayer performed with sincerity and Khushu (humility) accumulates spiritual wealth in the Hereafter. The rewards of Salah are immeasurable, and each act of prostration brings the believer closer to Allah, both in this world and in the next.

On the **Day of Resurrection**, the importance of Salah will be magnified beyond what we can comprehend in this world. It is narrated that **Salah will serve as a light** for the believer in the midst of the darkness and chaos of that day. The prayerful will be distinguished by their light, while those who neglected their prayers will find themselves in a state of profound regret. This stark contrast highlights the eternal significance of Salah as a source of salvation and guidance on the Day when no wealth or kin will avail.

The Qur'an speaks about the people of Hellfire and how one of their defining traits is their **neglect of prayer**. Allah tells us in Surah Al-Muddathir about the people of Saqar (one of the levels of Hell), who, when asked what led them there, will say: "We were not of those who prayed." This terrifying response underscores the weight of Salah in determining one's fate in the Hereafter. It also serves as a stern warning to those who take their prayers lightly or abandon them altogether.

For the believer, the performance of Salah with sincerity and Khushu is an act of **spiritual purification**. It cleanses the heart and soul, erasing sins and wrongdoings, much like a river washes away dirt from a person's body. Salah, performed consistently and correctly, builds a fortress of good deeds that will, insha'Allah, stand firm in the face of the trials and tests of the Day of Judgment.

The **reward of Salah** is not confined to the individual acts themselves. Each prayer contributes to the broader tapestry of a life lived in obedience to Allah. **Righteous deeds**, including Salah, serve as a means of securing one's place in Jannah (Paradise). Salah connects the believer to their ultimate purpose – worshipping Allah and striving for His pleasure. By maintaining Khushu and sincerity in Salah, the believer earns the greatest of all rewards: **the pleasure of Allah** and eternal bliss in the Hereafter.

One of the most beautiful rewards of Salah is that it brings the believer closer to **meeting Allah in Jannah**. The Prophet Muhammad (PBUH) mentioned that in Jannah, the believers will experience the ultimate joy: seeing their Lord. This honor is reserved for those who lived their lives in devotion to Him, particularly those who maintained their prayers. This meeting with Allah will surpass all the pleasures of the world, and it is the pinnacle of success in the Hereafter. Every time a believer prays, they are reminded of this ultimate goal, which keeps them motivated to worship consistently and sincerely.

The importance of **Fajr and Asr prayers** is specifically highlighted in many narrations, as these are times when angels record the deeds of humans and ascend to the heavens. Maintaining these prayers is a sign of true faith and commitment to Allah, and their rewards will be abundantly multiplied in the Hereafter.

It is also worth noting that Salah serves as a **means of intercession** on the Day of Judgment. The Prophet Muhammad (PBUH) stated that our prayers will speak on our behalf. When all worldly supports have vanished, and when even our closest relations may distance themselves from us, **our prayers will stand as witnesses** to our faith and submission. These prayers, if performed with Khushu and sincerity, will intercede for us, seeking mercy from Allah on our behalf.

Furthermore, the **reward of congregational prayer** is far greater than that of praying alone. The Prophet (PBUH) taught that praying in congregation increases the reward twenty-seven times. This increased reward is another way in which Salah paves the way to success in the Hereafter. The believer is encouraged to seek out opportunities to pray in congregation, thereby multiplying the rewards of their prayer and fostering a sense of unity and brotherhood in the Ummah (community).

In addition to the rewards, the Qur'an also describes how the **angels bear witness** to the prayer of the believers. These angels ascend to Allah, recording the good deeds of those who prayed with sincerity, adding to the believer's scale of good deeds. On the Day of Judgment, these recorded deeds will be brought forth, serving as testimony to the believer's dedication to Salah.

Khushu in Salah plays a pivotal role in securing the rewards of the afterlife. While all Salah is significant, the quality of the prayer matters greatly. Prayers offered with focus, sincerity, and humility are far more valuable than those performed mechanically or distractedly. Allah looks at the **heart of the worshiper** – at their intention, their submission, and their reverence for Him during the act of worship.

Salah is also a means by which the believer can achieve **peace and tranquility** in the Hereafter. Just as Khushu brings peace to the heart in this world, it will bring **eternal peace** in the life to come. This peace is a direct consequence of living a life centered on worshipping Allah, seeking His pleasure, and performing Salah with devotion. The comfort and serenity experienced in

Salah will translate into the ultimate peace of Jannah, where there will be no more sorrow, pain, or anxiety.

The **accountability** on the Day of Judgment will be intense, and the scales of deeds will be examined closely. Salah, when performed with sincerity and devotion, will be heavy on the scales, tipping them in favor of the believer. Allah's mercy is vast, and through the act of consistent and sincere prayer, the believer earns a place in Allah's mercy, which is the key to entering Jannah.

For the believer, the prospect of standing before Allah on the Day of Judgment is both awe-inspiring and sobering. **Salah prepares the heart and soul** for that moment of ultimate accountability. Every prostration is a reminder of the prostration to come, when every human being will bow before their Creator. This daily act of submission in Salah is a preparation for the moment when we will stand before Allah, with our deeds laid bare and our fate determined by His justice and mercy.

The **role of Salah in shaping the afterlife** is also evident in the way it trains the believer to be disciplined, patient, and focused. These qualities are essential for success in the Hereafter, where patience and perseverance in worship are rewarded with eternal bliss. Salah instills these qualities in the believer, ensuring that they are prepared not just for the trials of this life, but for the ultimate test of the Hereafter.

The **joy of Salah** lies in knowing that every prayer brings the believer closer to Allah. Each act of worship is a step toward the eternal reward of Jannah. This perspective transforms the act of prayer from a mere obligation into a source of hope, joy, and anticipation for the meeting with Allah in the Hereafter.

In the Hereafter, **Salah will be one of the key differentiators** between those who lived their lives with consciousness of Allah and those who neglected their duties. For those who upheld their prayers, the blessings of **Jannah** await. Every prayer recited with sincerity paves the path towards this eternal paradise. The Qur'an and Sunnah highlight that the inhabitants of **Jannah** are those who maintained their Salah and performed it with devotion and regularity. Their rewards are described in the most beautiful terms – rivers of milk and honey, gardens beneath which rivers flow, and eternal peace, free from the troubles of this world.

The **Prophet Muhammad (PBUH)** provided countless examples of how the righteous predecessors viewed their Salah in this life and its connection to the next. They treated it not as an optional act, but as the cornerstone of their existence. They viewed their prayers as **conversations with Allah**, moments where the veil between the servant and the Lord is lifted, and the mercy of Allah pours upon the believer.

This understanding led them to perform every prayer as though it could be their last. This attitude is something every believer must strive for – to pray as though the next moment might be their last on earth, preparing for the meeting with Allah in the Hereafter. It is this mindset that elevates a person's prayer, making it more sincere, more profound, and ultimately more valuable in the sight of Allah.

The **eternal rewards** of Salah also manifest in the believer's personal transformation. Those who pray regularly find that their lives take on a new level of **discipline, peace, and moral uprightness**. This internal transformation is the beginning of a much greater change that will be realized fully in the Hereafter. In essence, **Salah trains the soul** for Jannah. It is an exercise in humility, submission, and mindfulness of Allah. These are the very qualities that will be rewarded in the next life.

Salah is also a source of protection. The Qur'an repeatedly mentions that prayer acts as a shield, keeping the believer from **falling into sin and corruption**. On the Day of Judgment, this protection will be evident, as those who held fast to their prayers will find themselves shielded from the punishment that befalls those who neglected this essential duty. Salah acts as a **light and a barrier**, protecting the believer in both this life and the next.

The importance of Salah also extends to its ability to **unify the Ummah**. Congregational prayer, especially the Jumu'ah prayer and daily prayers in the masjid, brings believers together in worship, fostering a sense of unity, brotherhood, and collective responsibility. This unity is a reflection of the **greater unity** that will be experienced in Jannah, where the believers will be gathered together, free from division and discord. Thus, maintaining Salah in congregation is not only a means of earning rewards but also a preparation for the **eternal unity of the believers in Paradise**.

The **significance of Salah** in securing Allah's forgiveness is another essential aspect that ties it to the Hereafter. The Prophet Muhammad (PBUH) emphasized that **Salah erases sins**. Every time a believer stands in prayer, their minor sins are forgiven, and their hearts are purified. This continuous process of purification is crucial for the soul's journey to the Hereafter. Without constant repentance and purification, the heart becomes hardened, and the path to Jannah becomes more difficult.

In one narration, the Prophet (PBUH) compared **Salah to a river**. He said, "If one of you had a river at his door and bathed in it five times a day, would you notice any dirt on him?" The companions replied, "No." The Prophet then said, "This is the likeness of the five daily prayers. Allah erases sins with them." This shows the cleansing nature of Salah and how it **purifies the believer from the stains of sin**, ensuring that when they meet Allah, they do so with a clean slate.

For the believer, each prayer is an opportunity to **return to Allah** in repentance and humility. It is a chance to reflect on their actions, seek forgiveness, and make a fresh start. This constant cycle of sinning, repenting, and praying is what keeps the believer on the path of righteousness and ensures that their scale of good deeds outweighs their sins on the Day of Judgment.

In addition to spiritual purification, Salah instills in the believer a **sense of discipline** that extends beyond worship. The **regularity of prayer** – five times a day, without fail – teaches the believer the importance of time management, commitment, and responsibility. These qualities are crucial for achieving success not only in this life but also in the Hereafter. A disciplined person is one who prioritizes their duties to Allah, recognizing that everything else in life is secondary to their obligation to worship.

Moreover, Salah serves as a **reminder of the Hereafter**. Every time a believer stands in prayer, they are reminded that this world is temporary and that the ultimate goal is the **meeting with Allah** in the Hereafter. This constant reminder keeps the believer grounded and focused on what truly matters. It prevents them from becoming too attached to the fleeting pleasures of this world and encourages them to strive for the eternal rewards of the next.

This mindset is crucial for success in the Hereafter. Those who are constantly aware of the afterlife are more likely to **live their lives in accordance with Allah's commands**. They are more likely to avoid sin, seek forgiveness, and perform good deeds. Salah, therefore, serves as a **daily reminder** of the believer's ultimate purpose: to worship Allah and prepare for the Day of Judgment.

Salah's role in the Hereafter is not limited to the individual. It also has a profound impact on the community and the Ummah as a whole. A society that upholds Salah is one that is more likely to experience peace, justice, and harmony. Salah brings people together, creating a sense of unity and brotherhood that transcends race, nationality, and social status. This unity is a reflection of the **unity of the believers in Jannah**, where all will be gathered together in eternal bliss, free from the divisions and conflicts of this world.

In this way, Salah prepares not only the individual but also the community for the Hereafter. A community that prays together is one that is united in its devotion to Allah and its commitment to living according to His commands. This unity will be rewarded in the Hereafter, where the believers will be **gathered together in Paradise**, enjoying the rewards of their collective worship.

Moreover, Salah serves as a **means of strengthening the bonds** between individuals. When believers pray together, they are reminded of their shared faith and their shared goal of attaining Allah's pleasure. This shared experience fosters a sense of mutual responsibility and support, which is crucial for the well-being of the community. In the Hereafter, these bonds will be further strengthened, as the believers will be united in their eternal reward.

The **effects of neglecting Salah** are severe, both in this world and in the Hereafter. Those who abandon their prayers not only risk **losing the spiritual and moral benefits** that come with Salah, but they also risk being deprived of Allah's mercy on the Day of Judgment. The Qur'an is explicit in its warning to those who neglect their prayers, stating that **Hellfire awaits** those who fail to fulfill this obligation. The Prophet Muhammad (PBUH) also emphasized that the difference between a believer and a non-believer is the prayer. Neglecting Salah, therefore, puts a person at risk of falling into disbelief.

For those who have neglected their prayers, it is never too late to **repent and return to Allah**. The door of repentance is always open, and Allah's mercy is vast. The believer must make a sincere commitment to return to their prayers and strive to make up for the prayers they have missed. This is the path to securing Allah's forgiveness and ensuring that their place in the Hereafter is not compromised.

However, it is essential to recognize that repentance must be **accompanied by action**. Simply feeling remorse for missed prayers is not enough. The believer must actively seek to make up for those prayers, whether through voluntary prayers (Nafl) or by performing missed obligatory prayers (Qadha). This shows a true commitment to returning to Allah and securing His forgiveness.

The impact of **consistent Salah** is not only felt in the Hereafter but also deeply transforms one's life in this world. Salah becomes the very compass that guides the believer through the chaos and complexities of life. The five daily prayers act as a **constant reminder of one's purpose**. For someone who prays regularly, the trials and tribulations of the world take on a different meaning. Salah instills a sense of calm and peace, knowing that there is a higher power in control. It reminds the believer that nothing happens without Allah's will, and this faith allows them to face life's difficulties with a sense of grace and patience.

Every prostration brings with it a moment of surrender. The heart, which often becomes restless due to worldly concerns, finds rest in Salah. As the Prophet (PBUH) said, **"The comfort of my eyes has been placed in Salah."** It is in this prayer that a person is reminded of their dependency on Allah and their helplessness without Him. This realization leads to a spiritual renewal, an opportunity to reset one's intentions and focus on what truly matters.

Moreover, the connection that is established with Allah through Salah **strengthens a person's resilience** against the temptations and distractions of life. It is through this prayer that one develops the ability to recognize the **temporary nature of worldly success** and failures, focusing instead on the eternal rewards promised in the Hereafter. Thus, Salah becomes a guiding light that helps one navigate the ups and downs of life with the correct perspective.

The essence of Salah is not merely in the physical movements but in the **heart's submission**. It is a complete act of worship that involves the body, the heart, and the soul. While the body moves through the acts of standing, bowing, and prostrating, the heart is engaged in a conversation with its

Creator, expressing its deepest fears, hopes, and desires. Salah is a moment when the believer stands in front of Allah, speaking directly to Him. This moment of **intimate connection** is an unparalleled experience of peace and submission.

One of the key elements that transform a person's prayer from a mechanical act into a spiritual experience is **khushu' (humility)**. Khushu' in Salah means that the heart is present and engaged, fully aware of the greatness of Allah and the significance of the act of worship. The Qur'an praises those who establish their prayers with khushu', promising them success in both this world and the Hereafter.

It is this sense of humility that leads to **greater sincerity** in prayer. When a believer prays with khushu', they are not just fulfilling an obligation, but they are standing before Allah with complete awareness of His majesty and mercy. This awareness leads to a profound sense of awe, which makes the prayer more meaningful. In every action – from the opening Takbeer to the final Tasleem – the believer is reminded of their position as a humble servant of Allah.

As the believer develops **khushu'**, they also begin to experience the **transformative power** of Salah in other areas of their life. This transformation is not limited to the moments of prayer but extends to how they interact with the world around them. **Patience, compassion, and humility** become more pronounced traits, as the believer internalizes the lessons learned in Salah. The constant reminder of standing before Allah five times a day helps the individual maintain a sense of perspective, ensuring that their actions reflect the values they profess in their prayers.

This internal transformation has external manifestations. The believer who prays with sincerity and humility becomes more mindful of their behavior. They are careful with their words, gentle in their actions, and merciful in their dealings with others. This outward display of good character is a reflection of the **spiritual nourishment** they receive from their prayers. Salah acts as a daily purification for the soul, cleansing it from the impurities of pride, anger, and selfishness.

Additionally, the practice of **regular Salah** instills in the believer a deep sense of gratitude. Each prayer is an opportunity to thank Allah for the countless blessings He has bestowed upon them. Gratitude becomes a central theme in their lives, and this sense of gratitude extends beyond the prayer mat into their daily interactions with others. This shift in perspective – from focusing on what one lacks to being thankful for what one has – brings about a profound sense of contentment and peace.

Another significant benefit of **maintaining Salah** is that it serves as a **protection against sin**. The Qur'an explicitly mentions that prayer prevents a person from engaging in immoral and sinful behavior. This is because when a person prays consistently, they are reminded of Allah's presence and His watchfulness over them. The act of regularly bowing and prostrating before Allah instills a sense of accountability, making it difficult for the person to commit sins with the same ease as before.

This **shielding effect** of Salah is one of its most profound benefits. It is as though each prayer reinforces a protective barrier around the believer, keeping them safe from the traps of Shaytan and the distractions of the world. When a person is committed to their prayers, they become more vigilant over their actions and thoughts, knowing that they will stand before Allah soon, perhaps within a few hours, to answer for their deeds.

The **discipline of prayer** also helps in regulating a person's desires and inclinations. With Salah as a constant reminder, the believer learns to control their impulses, practicing self-restraint and patience. This self-control is not only beneficial in the context of avoiding sin, but it also has a ripple effect on other aspects of the believer's life, such as their **emotional stability, relationships, and personal goals**. The person who controls their desires and actions in accordance with Allah's commands finds greater success in both this life and the Hereafter.

The importance of **time management** in Islam is evident through the structure of Salah. The five daily prayers are spaced throughout the day, serving as a reminder of the importance of using one's time wisely. Salah teaches the believer that time is a precious resource, one that should not be wasted. This lesson becomes even more critical when viewed in light of the Hereafter. Every moment spent in heedlessness is a moment lost, while every moment spent in the remembrance of Allah is an investment in the eternal life to come.

Through this framework of **punctuality and discipline**, the believer becomes more conscious of how they spend their time. They learn to balance their worldly responsibilities with their religious obligations, ensuring that neither is neglected. This balance is essential for success in both worlds. While the believer is encouraged to seek a livelihood and enjoy the blessings of this life, they are constantly reminded that their ultimate goal is to prepare for the Hereafter.

The **regularity of prayer** also cultivates a sense of inner peace. No matter how chaotic life becomes, the believer knows that they will soon stand before Allah in prayer, where they can find solace and comfort. This regular connection with Allah becomes an anchor, grounding the believer in times of difficulty and giving them the strength to persevere. It is in these moments of prayer that the believer finds clarity, recognizing that their true purpose lies in serving Allah and seeking His pleasure.

Salah is not only a personal act of worship but also a **communal one**. The Prophet Muhammad (PBUH) emphasized the importance of praying in congregation, particularly for the men of the Ummah. The reward for praying in congregation is far greater than praying alone, and it fosters a sense of unity and brotherhood among the believers. When people pray together, they are reminded of their shared faith and their collective responsibility to uphold the teachings of Islam.

The act of praying in congregation is a reflection of the **larger community of believers**. Just as they stand together in prayer, shoulder to shoulder, they are also called to stand together in life, supporting one another in their struggles and joys. This sense of community is essential for the well-being of the Ummah, and Salah serves as the foundation for this unity. The bonds formed in prayer extend beyond the walls of the masjid, creating a network of support and solidarity that strengthens the entire Muslim community.

Furthermore, **praying in congregation** teaches humility. When believers stand side by side, there is no distinction between the rich and the poor, the educated and the uneducated, or the leader and the follower. All are equal before Allah, united in their worship of Him. This act of collective humility serves as a powerful reminder of the equality of all people before their Creator, fostering a sense of compassion and empathy within the community.

The **impact of congregational prayer** on the individual and the community is profound. Not only does it foster unity and humility, but it also strengthens the bond between the individual and Allah. When a person consistently prays in congregation, they are surrounded by other believers who are striving towards the same goal: seeking Allah's pleasure. This collective effort creates an environment of righteousness and encourages the individual to stay steadfast in their worship and obedience to Allah.

Moreover, the sense of **brotherhood and sisterhood** that is developed in the masjid extends into daily life. Muslims who pray together in congregation are more likely to support one another in times of need, offer advice and assistance, and help maintain each other's spiritual well-being. This interconnectedness creates a thriving, supportive community that works together to uphold the values of Islam. In many ways, congregational prayer serves as a reminder that the believer is never alone in their journey towards Allah.

For those who consistently attend the mosque for their prayers, there is an added benefit: a **sense of belonging**. The mosque becomes a spiritual sanctuary, a place where one can retreat from the distractions of the world and reconnect with their Creator. This sense of belonging fosters a deep love and attachment to the mosque, making it a place of solace, reflection, and spiritual growth. The Prophet (PBUH) mentioned that among those who will be shaded by Allah on the Day of Judgment is the one whose heart is attached to the mosque. This attachment not only strengthens one's relationship with Allah but also nurtures their bond with the community of believers.

The **final pillar of Salah's transformative power** lies in its ability to create a sense of purpose and direction in life. For the believer, every act of worship, every prostration, every prayer, serves as a reminder of their ultimate goal: to return to Allah in a state of purity and righteousness. Salah is the vehicle through which the believer continually renews their intention, seeking Allah's guidance and mercy at every turn.

Through this constant act of worship, the believer is reminded of their role as a servant of Allah, and this shapes their entire outlook on life. Rather than being consumed by worldly concerns and material pursuits, the believer is focused on achieving success in the Hereafter. This shift in perspective allows them to live a life of balance and purpose, where their actions are guided by the principles of Islam and their desire to please Allah.

Salah becomes more than just an act of worship; it becomes a way of life. It permeates every aspect of the believer's existence, from their relationships with others to their personal goals and ambitions. The **discipline and dedication** that Salah instills carry over into all areas of life, creating a sense of accountability and purpose that motivates the believer to strive for excellence in everything they do.

In conclusion, Salah is the heart of a believer's life. It is through this sacred act of worship that the believer finds peace, purpose, and a direct connection with Allah. The transformative power of Salah is undeniable, and for the one who prays with sincerity and humility, it becomes a source of strength, guidance, and ultimate success.

16: REVIVING SALAH IN OUR LIVES

Salah is not merely a ritualistic obligation that is performed five times a day; it is the foundation upon which a Muslim builds their relationship with Allah. However, to truly benefit from Salah, it must be revived in our hearts and souls. Reviving Salah means transforming it from a mere physical act into a spiritual journey that deepens our connection with our Creator. The first step in this revival is to realize that Salah is a gift from Allah. It is an opportunity for the believer to converse with Him directly, to seek forgiveness, guidance, and blessings.

The essence of this revival lies in understanding the gravity of standing before Allah. The believer must recognize that every Salah is a chance to present themselves to the Most Merciful, and this realization alone can transform their approach to prayer. The intention behind Salah should always be sincere, seeking Allah's pleasure alone, and not performed out of habit or social obligation. When this mindset is internalized, Salah becomes an act of liberation from worldly concerns, a moment where the heart finds peace in the remembrance of Allah.

One of the most effective ways to revive Salah is to reconnect with its meaning. Every word and every movement in Salah has a profound significance, and when understood, it elevates the prayer. For instance, the recitation of Surah Al-Fatiha is not just a collection of words but a conversation between the servant and their Lord. When the believer says, "Alhamdulillahi Rabbil 'Alamin" (All praise is for Allah, Lord of the worlds), they are acknowledging Allah's sovereignty over everything that exists. This declaration, when felt deeply, humbles the heart, making the servant realize their dependence on Allah in all matters.

Similarly, when we bow in Ruku, we declare the greatness of Allah. This physical act is a demonstration of our submission to His will, a reminder that despite our efforts, it is Allah who controls every outcome in our lives. Each part of Salah, from the Takbir to the final Tasleem, carries a meaning that, when contemplated upon, turns the prayer into a powerful spiritual experience.

Reviving Salah also means enhancing our physical and mental preparation before engaging in it. One of the key aspects is **wudhu** (ablution). Wudhu is not just a means of physical purification but also an act of spiritual cleansing. It is an opportunity to reflect upon one's sins and shortcomings, and to seek forgiveness before standing in the presence of Allah. The Prophet Muhammad (PBUH) said that when a believer performs wudhu, their sins are washed away with the water, until they are purified completely. Hence, making wudhu with mindfulness allows the believer to enter Salah with a heart that is already inclined towards repentance and humility.

Additionally, choosing a quiet and clean place to pray, free from distractions, can significantly improve one's focus during Salah. The environment in which we pray can influence our ability to maintain Khushu (humility and concentration), and it is for this reason that Muslims are encouraged to pray in clean, peaceful surroundings. A cluttered space can lead to a cluttered mind, whereas a serene and clean environment can help the heart find peace and focus on the remembrance of Allah.

Another essential element of reviving Salah is **consistency**. The Prophet (PBUH) emphasized the importance of performing good deeds consistently, even if they are small. This applies to Salah as well. The five daily prayers must be performed at their prescribed times, with sincerity and focus, for the believer to truly benefit from them. Consistency in Salah is not just about performing the obligatory prayers but also about building a routine that includes voluntary prayers (Nawafil), such as the Sunnah prayers, Tahajjud, and Duha.

The beauty of consistency in Salah is that it creates a spiritual rhythm in life. Just as the heart needs a steady rhythm to function properly, the soul needs the regularity of Salah to remain spiritually healthy. Each prayer serves as a reminder of our purpose in life and our duty towards Allah. This regularity also prevents the believer from falling into heedlessness, as they are constantly reminded of their relationship with Allah throughout the day.

The **mindset before prayer** plays a critical role in reviving Salah. It is important to approach prayer with the understanding that it is a privilege, not a burden. The believer must prepare themselves mentally by clearing their thoughts of worldly distractions and focusing solely on their intention to stand before Allah. A powerful way to achieve this mental readiness is by remembering that Salah is a direct connection with the Almighty, an opportunity to leave behind the stress and concerns of the dunya (worldly life) and find solace in the remembrance of Allah.

Additionally, reflecting on the rewards and virtues of Salah can serve as a motivating factor. The Prophet Muhammad (PBUH) mentioned that the first thing a person will be questioned about on the Day of Judgment is their Salah. If it is sound, the rest of their deeds will follow. This Hadith serves as a reminder that Salah is the key to success, both in this world and the Hereafter. When a person truly internalizes this, it transforms their attitude towards Salah, making it the most important part of their day.

A significant barrier to reviving Salah is **distraction**. In today's fast-paced world, the mind is often occupied with a multitude of concerns, making it difficult to focus during prayer. Overcoming distractions is crucial for attaining Khushu in Salah. One practical step is to consciously remind oneself of the greatness of Allah before beginning the prayer. This can be done through a few moments of silent reflection or by reciting some verses of the Quran that speak of Allah's majesty and power.

Furthermore, avoiding unnecessary distractions during prayer is essential. This means turning off devices, such as phones and other gadgets, that can interrupt the prayer. It is also important to choose a time for prayer when one is not overly tired or hungry, as these physical distractions can affect the quality of Salah. By removing these external and internal distractions, the believer creates an environment that is conducive to achieving Khushu.

In addition to minimizing distractions, the **physical posture** during prayer can greatly affect one's ability to focus. The Prophet (PBUH) emphasized the importance of performing the physical actions of Salah with calmness and precision. Each movement, from the standing posture to the prostration, should be performed with care and attention, as these actions themselves are acts of worship. Rushing through the prayer or performing the actions hastily diminishes the spiritual experience and prevents the believer from fully engaging with the prayer.

When a person performs Salah with slow, deliberate movements, they are more likely to focus on the meanings behind the actions. For example, the act of Ruku, where the believer bows down to acknowledge the greatness of Allah, should be performed with the awareness that this is an expression of submission and humility. The same applies to Sujood, where the believer places their forehead on the ground, the most humble position a human can take, in recognition of Allah's majesty. Performing these actions with mindfulness enhances the quality of Salah and helps the believer achieve true Khushu.

The **importance of Du'a (supplication)** in Salah should not be overlooked when seeking to revive one's prayer. After completing the obligatory recitations and actions of Salah, the time spent in Sujood or after the final Tasleem is an opportunity to engage in personal Du'a. The Prophet (PBUH) taught that during Sujood, the servant is closest to Allah, and it is in this position that Du'as are most likely to be accepted. This is a moment of immense spiritual intimacy between the believer and their Lord, and it should be used wisely to ask for guidance, forgiveness, and strength.

Making Du'a in one's own language, especially during voluntary prayers, can deepen the personal connection with Allah. It allows the believer to express their innermost feelings, fears, hopes, and aspirations. This level of personal engagement in Salah can transform it from a ritualistic act into a deeply spiritual experience that revives the heart and soul.

Consistency in **reciting and reflecting upon the Quran** during Salah is another way to revive the prayer. The Quran is the word of Allah, and reciting it during Salah allows the believer to engage directly with divine guidance. However, it is not enough to merely recite the words; it is essential to understand and reflect upon their meanings. For example, when reciting Surah Al-Fatiha, the believer should contemplate the meanings of Allah's attributes mentioned in the Surah, such as His mercy and lordship over all the worlds.

Reflecting on these attributes during prayer deepens the spiritual experience and reminds the believer of Allah's immense power and mercy. This reflection also helps in cultivating a sense of gratitude, humility, and reliance on Allah, which are essential components of Khushu. Additionally, varying the Surahs recited in prayer can prevent the prayer from becoming monotonous and help maintain focus.

In addition to reciting the Quran with reflection, one of the keys to reviving Salah is through **understanding the purpose behind each movement and action**. Each step in Salah holds a deeper spiritual significance that reflects the relationship between the servant and Allah. When the believer says "Allahu Akbar" (Allah is the Greatest) at the beginning of the prayer, they are acknowledging that nothing in the world is greater than Allah. This declaration, when internalized, puts into perspective the trivial nature of worldly concerns and helps the believer focus solely on the act of worship.

Similarly, the posture of Ruku symbolizes humility before Allah. The act of bowing is a physical manifestation of submission, acknowledging Allah's greatness and our dependence on Him. When the believer rises from Ruku, proclaiming, "Sami'Allahu liman hamidah" (Allah hears those who praise Him), they are reminded that Allah is always listening, ever-attentive to their prayers and supplications. These meanings transform the physical actions of Salah into a dynamic conversation with Allah, where every movement is filled with purpose.

The **emotional and mental state** of a person before Salah can greatly influence the quality of their prayer. It is essential to enter Salah with a heart that is present and a mind that is focused. A powerful method to achieve this is through making a conscious effort to disconnect from the stresses and distractions of daily life before starting the prayer. Engaging in a few moments of silent contemplation or Dhikr (remembrance of Allah) can help clear the mind and prepare the heart for Salah.

Moreover, remembering that Salah is not just an obligation but a moment of mercy from Allah changes the mindset entirely. The believer should approach each Salah as an opportunity to gain closeness to Allah, to seek His guidance, and to express gratitude for His countless blessings. When the heart is filled with these intentions, it becomes easier to attain Khushu, and Salah transforms into a moment of peace and connection, rather than a routine task.

Another significant aspect of reviving Salah is **making time for voluntary prayers** (Nawafil). While the five daily prayers are obligatory, the voluntary prayers serve to fill any shortcomings in the obligatory ones and bring additional rewards. The Prophet Muhammad (PBUH) consistently encouraged his followers to perform these extra prayers, particularly during times like Tahajjud (the night prayer) and Duha (the morning prayer). These prayers, although not obligatory, hold immense spiritual value and can greatly enhance one's relationship with Allah.

Tahajjud, for example, is a time when the believer stands before Allah in the stillness of the night, away from distractions, to engage in heartfelt supplication and worship. It is a time when the doors of mercy are wide open, and Allah descends to the lowest heaven, asking, "Is there anyone who is asking so that I may give them?" Voluntary prayers like these nurture the soul, strengthen one's Iman (faith), and bring the believer closer to Allah in ways that obligatory prayers alone may not achieve.

The **power of intention** in Salah is a profound concept that cannot be overlooked when aiming to revive the prayer. The intention, or Niyyah, behind every act of worship plays a crucial role in determining its sincerity and acceptance. When approaching Salah, it is important to renew one's intention, reminding oneself that this act is solely for the pleasure of Allah, not for the approval or recognition of others. Sincerity in Salah, also known as Ikhlas, is the essence of worship.

The Prophet Muhammad (PBUH) emphasized the importance of intentions by stating, "Actions are judged by intentions, and everyone will be rewarded according to what they intended." This principle serves as a reminder that Salah, performed with a pure heart and a sincere intention, holds immense spiritual value, even if it is not perfect in its execution. The believer should focus on perfecting their intention before Salah, ensuring that they are praying with the sole purpose of seeking closeness to Allah.

For those struggling to maintain consistency and focus in Salah, it can be helpful to **set realistic spiritual goals**. Rather than expecting to achieve perfect Khushu immediately, the believer should work towards gradual improvement. This can involve setting goals such as increasing concentration during specific parts of the prayer, memorizing new Surahs to recite, or reflecting more deeply on the meanings of certain verses. Each small step brings the believer closer to experiencing true humility and presence in Salah.

It is also important to remember that Allah is merciful and understands the struggles of His servants. He appreciates every sincere effort, even if the results are not immediate. The key is persistence and not giving up. Each attempt to improve one's Salah, no matter how small, is a step towards attaining a stronger connection with Allah. Over time, these efforts accumulate, leading to a more meaningful and spiritually fulfilling prayer experience.

The **company we keep** can also have a profound impact on the quality of our Salah. Surrounding oneself with individuals who are mindful of their prayers can serve as a powerful reminder to maintain one's own Salah with care and dedication. Good company encourages us to prioritize our relationship with Allah, while negative influences can lead us astray. The Prophet Muhammad (PBUH) said, "A man follows the religion of his friend; so each one should consider whom he makes his friend."

Praying in congregation, especially in the mosque, also has great spiritual benefits. The rewards of praying in congregation are multiplied, and the sense of community serves as a reminder of the collective responsibility of worship. When surrounded by others who are equally committed to Salah, the believer is more likely to remain consistent and focused in their own prayers. Additionally, attending the mosque regularly fosters a sense of belonging and motivates the believer to perform their Salah with greater sincerity and commitment.

For many, **understanding the consequences of neglecting Salah** can be a powerful motivator to revive it in their lives. The Prophet (PBUH) warned against the dangers of abandoning Salah, stating that it is the defining line between faith and disbelief. Salah is the most fundamental act of worship in Islam, and neglecting it can have serious spiritual consequences. When a person consistently misses their prayers, they are severing their connection with Allah and distancing themselves from His mercy and guidance.

Understanding the severity of missing Salah can serve as a wake-up call for those who may have become lax in their prayers. It is crucial to remember that Allah is always ready to forgive, but the responsibility lies on the individual to make an effort to turn back to Him. The beauty of Islam is that no matter how far a person has strayed, they can always return to Allah through sincere repentance and a renewed commitment to prayer.

The role of Dua (supplication) in reviving Salah is essential. Dua is the weapon of the believer, and it should be used to seek help in improving one's prayers. The Prophet Muhammad (PBUH) regularly made Dua for guidance in all aspects of life, including Salah. One of the Duas he made frequently was, "O Allah, help me to remember You, to be grateful to You, and to worship You in an excellent manner." This shows that even the most pious of people sought Allah's assistance in perfecting their worship.

Believers should make it a habit to ask Allah for help in achieving Khushu in Salah, in staying consistent with their prayers, and in strengthening their connection with Him. This humility in recognizing our own weaknesses and asking Allah for help is a key part of the spiritual journey. It is a reminder that, no matter how much effort we put into improving our Salah, we are always in need of Allah's guidance and support.

The **impact of Salah on daily life** is undeniable for those who establish it with sincerity and consistency. Salah is not just a momentary act of worship; it has the power to transform a person's entire outlook on life. When Salah is performed with mindfulness and humility, it instills a sense of discipline, peace, and purpose. The five daily prayers serve as a constant reminder of the believer's higher purpose, helping them navigate the challenges of life with a sense of clarity and trust in Allah.

Furthermore, Salah has the power to purify the heart and strengthen one's character. The regular remembrance of Allah keeps the believer mindful of their actions, preventing them from engaging in sinful behavior. The Prophet (PBUH) said, "Verily, the prayer prevents immorality and wrongdoing." This highlights the transformative power of Salah, which, when performed properly, can act as a shield against the temptations of this world and help the believer stay on the straight path.

For Salah to truly have a transformative impact, it is important to **remain patient and steadfast** in the journey towards improving it. Like any aspect of personal growth, developing Khushu and consistency in Salah takes time and effort. There will be moments of struggle, where concentration seems impossible or distractions seem overwhelming. In these moments, the believer must remember that every small step counts, and that Allah rewards perseverance.

Patience in Salah is not just about remaining focused during the prayer itself but also about being patient with oneself in the process of spiritual growth. Progress may be slow, but it is important to remain committed to the journey. The ultimate goal is to establish a deep and meaningful connection with Allah through Salah, and this is a journey that continues throughout one's life.

In addition to reciting the Quran with reflection, one of the keys to reviving Salah is through **understanding the purpose behind each movement and action**. Each step in Salah holds a deeper spiritual significance that reflects the relationship between the servant and Allah. When the believer says "Allahu Akbar" (Allah is the Greatest) at the beginning of the prayer, they are acknowledging that nothing in the world is greater than Allah. This declaration, when internalized, puts into perspective the trivial nature of worldly concerns and helps the believer focus solely on the act of worship.

Similarly, the posture of Ruku symbolizes humility before Allah. The act of bowing is a physical manifestation of submission, acknowledging Allah's greatness and our dependence on Him. When the believer rises from Ruku, proclaiming, "Sami'Allahu liman hamidah" (Allah hears those who praise Him), they are reminded that Allah is always listening, ever-attentive to their prayers and supplications. These meanings transform the physical actions of Salah into a dynamic conversation with Allah, where every movement is filled with purpose.

The **emotional and mental state** of a person before Salah can greatly influence the quality of their prayer. It is essential to enter Salah with a heart that is present and a mind that is focused. A powerful method to achieve this is through making a conscious effort to disconnect from the stresses and distractions of daily life before starting the prayer. Engaging in a few moments of silent contemplation or Dhikr (remembrance of Allah) can help clear the mind and prepare the heart for Salah.

Moreover, remembering that Salah is not just an obligation but a moment of mercy from Allah changes the mindset entirely. The believer should approach each Salah as an opportunity to gain closeness to Allah, to seek His guidance, and to express gratitude for His countless blessings. When the heart is filled with these intentions, it becomes easier to attain Khushu, and Salah transforms into a moment of peace and connection, rather than a routine task.

Another significant aspect of reviving Salah is **making time for voluntary prayers** (Nawafil). While the five daily prayers are obligatory, the voluntary prayers serve to fill any shortcomings in the obligatory ones and bring additional rewards. The Prophet Muhammad (PBUH) consistently encouraged his followers to perform these extra prayers, particularly during times like Tahajjud (the night prayer) and Duha (the morning prayer). These prayers, although not obligatory, hold immense spiritual value and can greatly enhance one's relationship with Allah.

Tahajjud, for example, is a time when the believer stands before Allah in the stillness of the night, away from distractions, to engage in heartfelt supplication and worship. It is a time when the doors of mercy are wide open, and Allah descends to the lowest heaven, asking, "Is there anyone who is asking so that I may give them?" Voluntary prayers like these nurture the soul, strengthen one's Iman (faith), and bring the believer closer to Allah in ways that obligatory prayers alone may not achieve.

The **power of intention** in Salah is a profound concept that cannot be overlooked when aiming to revive the prayer. The intention, or Niyyah, behind every act of worship plays a crucial role in determining its sincerity and acceptance. When approaching Salah, it is important to renew one's intention, reminding oneself that this act is solely for the pleasure of Allah, not for the approval or recognition of others. Sincerity in Salah, also known as Ikhlas, is the essence of worship.

The Prophet Muhammad (PBUH) emphasized the importance of intentions by stating, "Actions are judged by intentions, and everyone will be rewarded according to what they intended." This principle serves as a reminder that Salah, performed with a pure heart and a sincere intention, holds immense spiritual value, even if it is not perfect in its execution. The believer should focus on perfecting their intention before Salah, ensuring that they are praying with the sole purpose of seeking closeness to Allah.

For those struggling to maintain consistency and focus in Salah, it can be helpful to **set realistic spiritual goals**. Rather than expecting to achieve perfect Khushu immediately, the believer should work towards gradual improvement. This can involve setting goals such as increasing concentration during specific parts of the prayer, memorizing new Surahs to recite, or reflecting more deeply on the meanings of certain verses. Each small step brings the believer closer to experiencing true humility and presence in Salah.

It is also important to remember that Allah is merciful and understands the struggles of His servants. He appreciates every sincere effort, even if the results are not immediate. The key is persistence and not giving up. Each attempt to improve one's Salah, no matter how small, is a step towards attaining a stronger connection with Allah. Over time, these efforts accumulate, leading to a more meaningful and spiritually fulfilling prayer experience.

The **company we keep** can also have a profound impact on the quality of our Salah. Surrounding oneself with individuals who are mindful of their prayers can serve as a powerful reminder to maintain one's own Salah with care and dedication. Good company encourages us to prioritize our relationship with Allah, while negative influences can lead us astray. The Prophet Muhammad (PBUH) said, "A man follows the religion of his friend; so each one should consider whom he makes his friend."

Praying in congregation, especially in the mosque, also has great spiritual benefits. The rewards of praying in congregation are multiplied, and the sense of community serves as a reminder of the collective responsibility of worship. When surrounded by others who are equally committed to Salah, the believer is more likely to remain consistent and focused in their own prayers. Additionally, attending the mosque regularly fosters a sense of belonging and motivates the believer to perform their Salah with greater sincerity and commitment.

For many, **understanding the consequences of neglecting Salah** can be a powerful motivator to revive it in their lives. The Prophet (PBUH) warned against the dangers of abandoning Salah, stating that it is the defining line between faith and disbelief. Salah is the most fundamental act of worship in Islam, and neglecting it can have serious spiritual consequences. When a person consistently misses their prayers, they are severing their connection with Allah and distancing themselves from His mercy and guidance.

Understanding the severity of missing Salah can serve as a wake-up call for those who may have become lax in their prayers. It is crucial to remember that Allah is always ready to forgive, but the responsibility lies on the individual to make an effort to turn back to Him. The beauty of Islam is that no matter how far a person has strayed, they can always return to Allah through sincere repentance and a renewed commitment to prayer.

The role of Dua (supplication) in reviving Salah is essential. Dua is the weapon of the believer, and it should be used to seek help in improving one's prayers. The Prophet Muhammad (PBUH) regularly made Dua for guidance in all aspects of life, including Salah. One of the Duas he made frequently was, "O Allah, help me to remember You, to be grateful to You, and to worship You in an excellent manner." This shows that even the most pious of people sought Allah's assistance in perfecting their worship.

Believers should make it a habit to ask Allah for help in achieving Khushu in Salah, in staying consistent with their prayers, and in strengthening their connection with Him. This humility in recognizing our own weaknesses and asking Allah for help is a key part of the spiritual journey. It is a reminder that, no matter how much effort we put into improving our Salah, we are always in need of Allah's guidance and support.

The **impact of Salah on daily life** is undeniable for those who establish it with sincerity and consistency. Salah is not just a momentary act of worship; it has the power to transform a person's entire outlook on life. When Salah is performed with mindfulness and humility, it instills a sense of discipline, peace, and purpose. The five daily prayers serve as a constant reminder of the believer's higher purpose, helping them navigate the challenges of life with a sense of clarity and trust in Allah.

Furthermore, Salah has the power to purify the heart and strengthen one's character. The regular remembrance of Allah keeps the believer mindful of their actions, preventing them from engaging in sinful behavior. The Prophet (PBUH) said, "Verily, the prayer prevents immorality and wrongdoing." This highlights the transformative power of Salah, which, when performed properly, can act as a shield against the temptations of this world and help the believer stay on the straight path.

For Salah to truly have a transformative impact, it is important to **remain patient and steadfast** in the journey towards improving it. Like any aspect of personal growth, developing Khushu and consistency in Salah takes time and effort. There will be moments of struggle, where concentration seems impossible or distractions seem overwhelming. In these moments, the believer must remember that every small step counts, and that Allah rewards perseverance.

Patience in Salah is not just about remaining focused during the prayer itself but also about being patient with oneself in the process of spiritual growth. Progress may be slow, but it is important to remain committed to the journey. The ultimate goal is to establish a deep and meaningful connection with Allah through Salah, and this is a journey that continues throughout one's life.

In conclusion, reviving Salah in our lives is a journey that requires intention, effort, and consistency. It begins with a sincere desire to strengthen one's relationship with Allah and continues with small, intentional steps towards improvement. From understanding the deeper meanings of the words and actions in Salah to making time for voluntary prayers and asking Allah for help, each effort brings the believer closer to achieving Khushu and a more fulfilling spiritual experience.

ABOUT THE AUTHOR

Aman Maqsood is a dedicated writer, speaker, and student of Islamic sciences with a passion for rekindling the spiritual essence of prayer in the hearts of Muslims. His works focus on nurturing a deep, personal relationship with Allah through the act of Salah, grounded in the timeless teachings of the Qur'an and Sunnah.

Drawing from the rich legacy of **Manhaj-e-Salaf**, Aman emphasizes the importance of Tawheed and the spiritual dimensions of worship in daily life. His goal is to help Muslims reconnect with their faith, experience the transformative power of Salah, and cultivate sincerity, humility, and mindfulness in their worship.

"As a humble student of knowledge. I (Aman Maqsood) welcome any feedback or corrections. **I am human** and capable of making mistakes. I strive my utmost to ensure that everything I share aligns with the Qur'an and Sunnah. However, if any part of this work inadvertently goes against authentic Islamic teachings, I ask for your forgiveness. Please do not follow my words if they conflict with the teachings of Islam, and I humbly request that you inform me so that I can correct any errors immediately, inshaAllah, as long as I am alive. Feel free to email me at **aman.mk2013@gmail.com** for any corrections or insights." – Aman Maqsood

Aman's writing draws inspiration from the manhaj-e-salaf, focusing on authentic Islamic teachings, and his works resonate with readers looking for guidance grounded in tradition yet applicable to contemporary life. Through his books, workshops, and digital content, Aman Maqsood encourages a return to the essence of Islam: pure Tawheed, devotion to Allah, and the pursuit of truth.

Want to stay connected and receive free valuable content? Scan the QR code below to access exclusive insights, free eBooks, and other resources that will deepen your understanding of Islam. As a thank you for joining my community, I'm offering a **free, exclusive guide** to help you enhance your personal faith journey

@IQRAJOURNEY